Mathematical Thinking and Learning

An International Journal

Volume 7, Number 1, 2005

Special Issue:
Advanced Mathematical Thinking
Guest Editors:
Annie Selden and John Selden

Contents

Journal Information

Subscriptions: *Mathematical Thinking and Learning: An International Journal* is published quarterly by Lawrence Erlbaum Associates, Inc., 10 Industrial Avenue, Mahwah, NJ 07430–2262. Subscriptions for the 2004 volume are available only on a calendar-year basis.

Individual rates: **Print *Plus* Online:** $60.00 in US/Canada, $90 outside US/Canada. Institutional rates: **Print-Only:** $420.00 in US/Canada, $450.00 outside US/Canada. **Online-Only:** $395.00 in US/Canada and outside US/Canada. **Print *Plus* Online:** $440.00 in US/Canada, $470.00 outside US/Canada. Visit LEA's Web site at http://www.erlbaum.com to view a free sample.

Order subscriptions through the Journal Subscription Department, Lawrence Erlbaum Associates, Inc., 10 Industrial Avenue, Mahwah, NJ 07430–2262.

Claims: Claims for missing copies cannot be honored beyond 4 months after mailing date. Duplicate copies cannot be sent to replace issues not delivered due to failure to notify publisher of change of address.

Change of Address: Send address changes to the Journal Subscription Department, Lawrence Erlbaum Associates, Inc., 10 Industrial Avenue, Mahwah, NJ 07430–2262.

Permissions: Special requests for permission should be sent to the Permissions Department, Lawrence Erlbaum Associates, Inc., 10 Industrial Avenue, Mahwah, NJ 07430–2262.

Abstracts/Indexes: This journal is abstracted or indexed in *PsycINFO/Psychological Abstracts; Zentralblatt für Mathematik/Mathematics Abstracts; ERIC Clearinghouse for Science, Mathematics, and Environmental Education; Current Index to Journals in Education; EBSCOhost Products; Education Index; Education Abstracts; Australian Education Index; Education Research Abstracts; and Contents Pages in Education.*

Microform Copies: Microform copies of this journal are available through ProQuest Information and Learning, P.O. Box 1346, Ann Arbor, MI 48106–1346. For more information, call 1–800–521–0600, ext. 2888.

Visit LEA's website at **http://www.erlbaum.com**

Printed in the United States of America   ISSN 1098–6065

MATHEMATICAL THINKING AND LEARNING, 7(1), 1–13

Perspectives on Advanced Mathematical Thinking

Annie Selden and John Selden
Department of Mathematical Sciences
New Mexico State University

This article sets the stage for the following 3 articles. It opens with a brief history of attempts to characterize *advanced mathematical thinking,* beginning with the deliberations of the Advanced Mathematical Thinking Working Group of the International Group for the Psychology of Mathematics Education. It then locates the articles within 4 recurring themes: (a) the distinction between identifying kinds of thinking that might be regarded as advanced at any grade level, and taking as advanced any thinking about mathematical topics considered advanced; (b) the utility of characterizing such thinking for integrating the entire curriculum; (c) general tests, or criteria, for identifying advanced mathematical thinking; and (d) an emphasis on advancing mathematical practices. Finally, it points out some commonalities and differences among the 3 following articles.

This introduction and the following three articles discuss several diverse views of advanced mathematical thinking (AMT). We first provide a brief overview of the landscape, without developing any particular aspect in detail, and then locate these three articles within four recurring themes found in the growing literature. All three articles discuss ways of thinking about or doing mathematics that the authors consider beneficial for students. Sometimes referred to as "mathematical habits of mind" or "mathematical practices," these ways of thinking about and doing mathematics may be fairly widely regarded as productive, but are often left to the implicit curriculum. That is, they are usually not taught explicitly, and in current school curricula, may not be considered by teachers as part of their responsibility. Indeed, some teachers may not see such habits of mind as capable of being taught. Perhaps that is one reason the recent RAND Mathematics Study Panel advocated the teach-

---

Requests for reprints should be sent to Annie Selden, Dept. of Mathematical Sciences, New Mexico State University, Box 30001 Dept 3MB, Las Cruces, NM 88003–0001. E-mail: aselden@emmy.nmsu.edu

ing and learning of *mathematical practices* as one of three large focal areas for future research in mathematics education (Ball, 2003). We conclude with a brief comparison of the three articles.

We hope that by laying out some recurring themes in the discussions of AMT that further progress in designing and implementing curricula will be encouraged, and that by introducing aspects of advanced mathematical thinking or its precursors earlier, the K–16, or even the K–graduate school curricula can become better integrated. In this, we are encouraged by the most recent *NCTM Principles and Standards for School Mathematics* (2000) that recommend Problem Solving, Reasoning and Proof, Communication, Connections, and Representation Standards for all instructional programs from prekindergarten through Grade 12. These process standards include the recommendation that all instructional programs should enable students to: (a) apply and adapt a variety of appropriate strategies to solve problems; (b) select and use various types of reasoning and methods of proof; (c) analyze and evaluate the mathematical thinking and strategies of others; (d) understand how mathematical ideas interconnect; and (e) select, apply, and translate among mathematical representations to solve problems. Parts of the discussions of AMT in this issue can be interpreted as if they were an attempt to come to a better understanding of what these five NCTM recommendations mean, and perhaps, also to supplement them.

A BRIEF HISTORY

From initial considerations thereof, the term *advanced mathematical thinking* has been fraught with ambiguity—does the term *advanced* refer to the mathematics, or to the thinking, or to both? Clearly, more advanced topics in the curriculum, such as calculus or differential equations, cannot be grasped without a solid understanding of more elementary topics, such as function and rate of change. These, in turn, depend on an understanding of proportion and number. Also, the thinking lies on a continuum—processes such as analyzing, conjecturing, defining, formalizing, proving, generalizing, and synthesizing, although more frequent in advanced mathematics, can and should develop from elementary grades onward (See Dreyfus, 1990).

Research into cognitive, and other aspects, of mathematical thinking and learning began with elementary topics, such as the acquisition of early number concepts. Indeed, research on more elementary concepts was predominant in the work of the International Group for the Psychology of Mathematics Education (PME) from its beginning in 1976 until the mid-1980s (Dreyfus, 1990). Then, in 1985, a PME Working Group on Advanced Mathematical Thinking was formed, and it continued meeting until the late-1990s. For practical purposes, when initial discussions failed to coalesce around a single satisfactory definition, this Working Group focused its efforts on the teaching and learning of mathematics at the tertiary level.[1]

Three products resulted from the deliberations of this PME Working Group: (a) a chapter on advanced mathematical thinking authored by Tommy Dreyfus in an International Commission on Mathematical Instruction Study Series volume featuring the work of PME (Nesher & Kilpatrick, 1990); (b) a volume that considered the nature of advanced mathematical thinking, cognitive theory, and overviews of research into the teaching and learning of such advanced topics as limits, differential equations, infinity, and proof (Tall, 1991); and (c) a special issue of *Educational Studies in Mathematics* devoted to advanced mathematical thinking (Dreyfus, 1995).

In the second of these, Tall (1991, p. 20) asserted that "The move from elementary to AMT involves a significant transition: that from *describing* to *defining*, from *convincing* to *proving* in a logical manner based on definitions." Expanding on this in a subsequent PME plenary address, Tall (1995) stated that cognitive growth from elementary to AMT can be hypothesized as starting "from 'perception of' and 'action on' objects in the external world, building through two parallel developments—one visuo-spatial to verbal-deductive, the other successive process-to-object encapsulations using manipulable symbols" (p. 63) leading eventually "from the equilibrium of visual conviction and proceptual manipulation to defined objects and formal deduction.... The full range of creative advanced mathematical thinking is mainly the province of professional mathematicians and their students" (p. 71).

Somewhat later, beginning in 1998, related issues were taken up by a Working Group of the North American Chapter of the International Group for the Psychology of Mathematics Education (PME–NA) titled, The Role of Advanced Mathematical Thinking in Mathematics Education Reform. This PME–NA Working Group began by discussing such questions as what kinds of earlier experiences might help students make the transition to the kinds of AMT that postsecondary students are often asked to engage in (Heid, Ferrini-Mundy, Graham, & Harel, 1998). This rather naturally metamorphosed into efforts at characterizing AMT and looking for seeds thereof that are, or could be, planted early in students' mathematical careers. For example, the tendency to interpret a concept in multiple ways can be useful for problem solving at various levels (Heid et al., 1999). Three perspectives emerged:

1. AMT deals with the kind of thinking that occurs mainly at the collegiate or graduate levels and requires precise reasoning about ideas that are not entirely accessible to the five senses. This view is expanded upon in the Edwards, Dubinsky, and McDonald article (this issue).

---

[1]This is our own observation, based on participating in all but the first few meetings of the Working Group.

2. A consideration of AMT as involving the overcoming of epistemological obstacles, together with ways of thinking that are helpful in this. This view has been extended to the current Harel and Sowder article (this issue).

3. A preference for focusing on "advancing mathematical activity" centered around expanded definitions of horizontal and vertical mathematizing (Treffers, 1987) as exemplified by the mathematical practices of symbolizing, algorithmatizing, and defining. This view has been expanded into the current Rasmussen, Zandieh, King, and Teppo article (this issue; see Heid, Harel, Ferrini-Mundy, & Graham, 2000).

Over the past 10 or so years, "advanced mathematical thinking" has come to be a descriptor, or key word, that authors can, and often do, use to describe their research for journals such as the *Journal for Research in Mathematics Education (JRME)*. As with all such descriptors, it is left to authors to determine which key words describe their research, and thus, the phrase has come to mean "whatever the author chooses it to mean" (E. Silver, past editor of *JRME*, personal communication, April 8, 2003). The main effect of this, perhaps resulting from authors taking their cue from the bulk of the research reported in Tall's (1991) seminal volume, seems to have been that the term is often used to signal mathematics education research at the tertiary level. Although Thompson (1993) titled his review of the Tall (1991) volume, *Yes, Virginia, Some Children Do Grow Up to Be Mathematicians*, he also noted that Tall had emphasized that "advanced mathematical thinking does not begin after high school" and that "this thinking must begin in the first grade." Pimm (1995), in his rather critical review of the Tall (1991) volume, observed that the adjective "advanced" had been applied, by the book's chapter authors, variously to describe both the mathematics and the thinking. Pimm, noting that one can always advance beyond the state one is currently in, questioned whether there is even such an entity as AMT.

That AMT should have something to do with the nature of advanced mathematics, toward which one can view elementary mathematics as aiming, as well as something to do with the practices of mathematicians, does not seem in doubt. However, exactly what features might characterize that mathematics and that thinking continues to be deliberated. Furthermore, exactly how one might foster such thinking in a seamless way so that the seeds, or precursors, of that thinking are planted and nurtured from early on is still an open question—a question addressed in this issue.

Although the *NCTM Principles and Standards for School Mathematics* (2000) advocate that the process standards (problem solving, reasoning and proof, communication, connections, and representation) be integrated across instructional programs from prekindergarten through Grade 12—in effect, that students' mathematical thinking should become progressively more advanced—accomplishing this is no easy task. However, there are some indications of how early exposure to challenging mathematical ideas can provide experiences upon which to draw for subsequent, sometimes much later, mathematical generalizations and abstractions (cf. Maher & Martino, 1996a, 1996b, 1997; Maher & Speiser, 1997).

What special kinds of thinking, by undergraduates, graduate students, and mathematicians are especially associated with advanced mathematics? Indeed, what kinds of mathematics might reasonably be regarded as advanced within the kindergarten through graduate school curricula?

FOUR RECURRING THEMES

Our review of the literature, together with the three articles herein, suggests four general themes regarding the nature of, and possible characterizations of, advanced mathematical thinking.

Advanced Thinking Versus Advanced Mathematics

The first theme concerns the distinction between, on the one hand, directly identifying the kinds of mathematical thinking that could be regarded as advanced at any age or grade level, and on the other hand, of taking as advanced the kinds of thinking characteristic of mathematical topics that could themselves be identified as advanced. For example, Edwards et al. (this issue) discuss this distinction in the introduction to their contribution. In practice, however, these two distinct points of view often support each other. That is, to argue that some kind of thinking, say the habits of mind and abilities associated with handling abstraction, is advanced, one can note that such thinking often occurs in thinking about advanced topics, such as abstract algebra. Conversely, if one needed to argue that abstract algebra was advanced, one might note that much of the thinking involved is indeed abstract.

The Utility of Characterizing Advanced Mathematical Thinking

A second theme concerns the utility of identifying or characterizing various kinds of AMT. Once a kind of thinking, such as generalizing, has been identified as advanced, it seems more likely that some form of it, or at least a precursor to it, could be analyzed and taught earlier in the kindergarten through graduate school curriculum. This would allow the curriculum to be better integrated by providing long-range goals for instruction that go beyond satisfying the mathematical needs of everyday life in a technological society. This theme appears to have played a considerable role in the development of the current *NCTM Principles and Standards for School Mathematics* (2000). There is also an "existence proof" of how a series of relatively small, but coherent, long-term interventions with one group of students over a number of years can lead to remarkable instances of AMT, including the development by students, on their own, of the idea of proof (Maher & Martino, 1996a, 1996b).

Consider the case of Stephanie, one of a number of children with whom Maher and Martino (1996a, 1996b, 1997) began their long-range, but occasional, interventions commencing in Grade 1. By Grade 3, the children had begun building physical models and justifying their solutions to the following problem: How many different towers of heights 3, 4, or 5 can be made using red and yellow blocks? Stephanie, not only justified her solutions, she validated or rejected

> her own ideas and the ideas of others on the basis of whether or not they made sense to her. ... She recorded her tower arrangements first by drawing pictures of towers and placing a single letter on each cube to represent its color, and then by inventing a notation of letters to represent the color cubes. (Maher & Speiser, 1997, p. 174)

She used spontaneous heuristics like guess and check, looking for patterns, and thinking of a simpler problem, and developed arguments to support proposed parts of solutions, and extensions thereof, to build more complete solutions. Occasional interventions continued for Stephanie through Grade 7. Then in Grade 8 she moved to another community and another school and her mathematics was a conventional algebra course. The researchers interviewed her that year about the coefficients of $(a + b)^2$ and $(a + b)^3$. About the latter, she said "So there's a cubed ... And there's three a squared b and there's three ab squared and there's b cubed. ... Isn't that the same thing?" Asked what she meant, she replied, "As the towers." It turned out, upon further questioning, that Stephanie had been visualizing red and yellow towers of height 3 to organize the products $a^i b^j$. (For a more complete discussion, see Maher & Speiser, 1997.) Stephanie then used the towers of blocks metaphor to develop the coefficients of expressions such as $(a + b + c)^n$, a remarkable achievement that prompted Speiser, upon presenting his paper at PME–21 in Lahti, Finland, to remark, "I wish some of my [university] students were able to reason that well."

Criteria for Advancedness

A third theme focuses on finding what could be called very general tests, or criteria, for identifying AMT that might be considered at many grade levels throughout the curriculum. Harel and Sowder (this issue) suggest such a very general test. Their central idea is that AMT involves, to some degree, at least one of the three characteristics of epistemological obstacles. An epistemological obstacle is a bit of knowledge, rather than a lack of knowledge, that somehow inherently stands in the way of acquiring subsequent, more general, knowledge. It is sufficiently robust to withstand occasional contradictions. Finally, such an obstacle should turn up in the historical development of mathematics. Harel and Sowder consider the influence of an epistemological obstacle to be a matter of degree and state that its influence is often blended with that of one or more didactic obstacles, that is, obstacles somehow arising from the teaching itself rather than from the nature of what is to be learned.

Edwards et al. (this issue) also take this tack, proposing a different, although not necessarily conflicting test. They develop the idea that thinking might be regarded as advanced if it depends on deductive reasoning and does not depend directly upon sensory perception. While they acknowledge that "exemplary mathematical thinking may occur at any age of student and level of mathematics," they wish to reserve the term "advanced mathematical thinking" for thinking that involves "rigorous and deductive reasoning about mathematical objects that are unavailable to our five senses." Although this kind of advancedness can occur at a number of levels and we have previously mentioned the remarkable degree to which young students can engage in deductive reasoning, it seems unlikely that such students would often reason about mathematical objects unavailable to the five senses. Indeed, we see students as slowly progressing from first tacitly viewing the objects of mathematics as part of, or closely associated with, the physical world, and consequently as possessing descriptive definitions. Eventually some students come to view mathematical objects as abstract and brought into existence by analytic definitions,[2] such as that of group in abstract algebra. To illustrate how mathematical objects might be seen at the beginning of such a progression, consider a mathematically naive individual observing 3 red apples. That there are 3 and that they are *red* would have, more or less, the same status, namely, that of properties of physical objects. Somewhat later, the number 3 might come to be seen as an object in its own right, but one that is part of, or associated with, the physical world. Such objects have descriptive definitions that should correctly mirror the corresponding physical objects or situations. These initial perspectives of mathematical objects, and their corresponding descriptive definitions, are quite different from perspectives taken much later when using

---

[2]Although analytic definitions can be inspired by physical situations, they are often considered as ultimately reducible to undefined terms; hence, one cannot regard them as right or wrong. By contrast, although descriptive, or synthetic, definitions describe existing objects or situations often associated with the physical world, such as democracy or whole number addition, they *can* be regarded as right or wrong. Moreover, when using an analytic definition, it is essential to attend to all parts of the definition. However, by contrast, although synthetic definitions often provide incomplete and redundant descriptions, it not always essential to attend to *all* parts of such definitions. Difficulties arising from undergraduate students treating mathematical definitions as descriptive, rather than analytic, have been described by Edwards and Ward (2004).

analytic definitions that, although they may be inspired by physical observations, are more or less reducible to undefined terms.[3]

The utility of the Edwards et al., idea of advanced mathematical thinking as "unavailable to the five senses," and the idea of a progression of students' views regarding the status of mathematical objects, can be illustrated by examining a suggestion offered at a recent seminar. We were discussing various systematic errors that some fourth- and fifth-grade pupils' make when comparing the size of decimal numbers (Resnick et al., 1989). The offered suggestion was: Why not simply avoid all of the cited problems by defining, and directly using, $x < y$ if and only if $x - y$ is negative? However, it seems unlikely that one could clear up pupils' difficulties stemming from their previous whole number and fraction knowledge by simply defining away the problem. As noted by Resnick et al. (1989), fourth- and fifth-grade pupils making such errors are likely to see decimals, and their comparisons, as extensions of whole numbers or fractions studied earlier. Thus, they are likely to see decimals as numbers derived from the physical world. For such pupils, whole numbers, fractions, and even decimals may be "out there" in the physical world, and as such, only capable of being described. Thus, for these pupils, it seems inappropriate to attempt to redefine the concept of "less than" by simply introducing this abstract, analytic definition. Trying to do so might result in making little change in how the pupils actually make decimal comparisons.

Advancing Mathematical Practices

Finally, a fourth theme consists of elucidating specific kinds of mathematical practices, together with describing the development of the associated thinking. One very general practice, that occurs across the K–16 curriculum and in the work of mathematicians, might be called *structuring* real world and mathematical problems. Mathematicians such as Hadamard (1945) and Thurston (1994) have tried, often through introspection, to understand their own, and other mathematicians' creative structuring processes. By structuring, we mean the introduction of notation, diagrams, definitions, analyses, etc., to a class of problems to facilitate their solution—in some cases by converting them to other kinds of problems. This may involve the creation of structures, for example, symbols new to the practitioners.

---

[3]One could ask: What is the utility of having students move from viewing the objects of mathematics as descriptively defined aspects of the physical world, to viewing them as analytically defined abstract objects? One answer is: In constructing and understanding proofs, it is essential to attend to *all* parts of a definition—something unnecessary for other kinds of arguments based on descriptive definitions of physical objects or situations. Another answer is: Mathematics today is exceptionally reliable—barring the later discovery of errors, when a theorem is proved, "it stays proved." This reliability, and indeed independence from place and time, depends not only on careful logic, but also on the use of analytic definitions. The kind of unreliability that can result from treating mathematical definitions as descriptive can be seen in *Proofs and Refutations* (Lakatos, 1976).

An example of structuring is provided by the mathematizing, in particular, the symbolizing, elucidated in the article by Rasmussen et al. (this issue). Starting with either a real world or a mathematical problem, mathematizing is a process of consideration and reflection that alternates between two forms—*horizontal*, during which the mathematics at hand becomes more familiar and is broadened, and *vertical*, during which new mathematics (notation, algorithms, definitions, etc.) is created. Such mathematizing can be seen especially well in the kind of inquiry-oriented classrooms, in which students routinely come to explain and justify their thinking, from which Rasmussen et al. (this issue) draw their examples. Although their article describes the mathematical activity of undergraduates, the authors propose that the notion of mathematizing that they develop is "not limited to grade or content levels."

Another more commonly taught kind of structuring is modeling that may not involve the creation of new mathematical objects. In the traditional view of modeling, a student typically starts with a problem in a familiar setting (real world or mathematical) and adds (or focuses on some aspect of) structure, such as variables, diagrams, equations, functions, etc., with a view to converting the given problem into a more tractable one in a (or another) familiar mathematical domain. For example, tertiary students might be asked to show that, in Euclidean geometry, angles cannot be trisected (using only straightedge and compass) first by converting the problem to one about fields, and then to one about Galois groups in the hope that the new problem might be easier to solve. Students are usually not asked to "see" for themselves the relationship between two such disparate domains as Euclidean geometry and abstract algebra. If students *are* asked to "see" for themselves such relationships, then even problems in applying first calculus (without explanations of how to solve them, or even whether to use calculus) can become nonroutine modeling problems.

That such "seeing" is difficult at any level can be observed in the work of Lobato and Siebert (2002) in the case of Terry, a student who had recently completed Algebra 1 in Grade 8. In a summer teaching experiment, Terry and other students were asked what measurements they would take to determine the steepness of a wheelchair ramp (without explicitly asking them to consider slope). Terry initially focused on the height of the ramp and considered its length to be a dependent variable. As it turned out, Terry's reasoning evolved through quite a number of stages (described in detail by the authors), and it took instructor-facilitation to get him to see steepness as a function of the two independently varying quantities, height and length. Perhaps in Terry's defense and certainly as a caution to others who might attempt a similar teaching experiment, the authors note that "there are five other ratios that also provide mathematically consistent, albeit unconventional, measures of steepness (namely slant height to length, slant height to height, length to height, height to slant height, and length to slant height)" making it less likely that "a student would naturally focus on the particular ratio of height to length" (p. 111).

In elucidating specific kinds of mathematical practices and the creative ways students might arrive at them, we suggest that examinations of structuring, and in particular, the examples of symbolizing, algorithmatizing, and defining in Rasmussen et al. (this issue), do not nearly exhaust the possibilities. Much of the mathematics education research literature at the undergraduate level, although not directly about the nature of advanced thinking, or couched in terms of mathematical practices, nevertheless suggests promising areas for investigation. For example, one of our articles (Selden & Selden, 2003) is about mid-level undergraduates' ability to check the correctness of proofs and the ways they go about it, but does not give a detailed delineation of the kind of practices or thinking involved. However, it does note that this complex kind of thinking, that we called *validation*, is widespread among mathematicians and suggests it may eventually be fairly well described. The empirical part of the study suggests that current mid-level U.S. university students are not good at validating proofs, but our experience suggests many graduate students and mathematicians can do so quite reliably. Thus, the article implicitly suggests that students who continue in mathematics need to improve the practice of validating proofs. While there is currently little direct instruction in this practice, students who learn to validate proofs on their own might be considered as engaged in a form of mathematizing.

Much of the literature at the undergraduate level provides similar indications of features of mathematical practices or thinking. This includes examinations of problem solving (Arcavi, Kessel, Meira, & Smith, 1998; Schoenfeld, 1985), studies of students dealing with definitions (Dahlberg & Housman, 1997; Edwards, 1997; Rasmussen & Zandieh, 2000), investigations of students dealing with such abstract algebra concepts as isomorphism and quotient group (Dubinsky, 1997; Leron, Hazzan, & Zazkis, 1995), considerations of reasoning in linear algebra (Sierpinska, Defence, Khatcherian, & Saldanha, 1997) and reflections on unifying and generalizing concepts (Dorier, 1995), among many others.

COMMONALITIES AND DIFFERENCES

In addition to locating the following articles in this issue within the four recurring themes—advanced thinking versus advanced mathematics, the utility of characterizing such thinking, criteria for advancedness, and advancing practices, it might be useful to compare them directly.

Harel and Sowder (this issue) have a very general test, or criterion, for AMT, namely that one should be able to see in a student's "way of thinking" at least one of the three characteristics of an epistemological obstacle. While such thinking refers to individual students, it is likely to occur in association with a wide variety of mathematical topics and at many levels throughout a student's entire mathematical education. For example, AMT is likely to occur not only in reasoning about higher dimensional vector spaces but also, much earlier, in proportional reasoning.

Edwards et al. (this issue) also have a very general test, but a different one. In their view, AMT depends on rigorous deductive reasoning about mathematical notions inaccessible to the five senses. Just as with Harel and Sowder (this issue), this kind of thinking refers to individuals, but is likely to occur in studying certain topics and at many levels. However, unlike Harel and Sowder, it is unlikely to occur very often during preuniversity studies. As with Harel and Sowder's view, such AMT is likely to occur in reasoning about higher dimensional vector spaces; however, in contrast to that view, it is unlikely to be involved in proportional reasoning.

Rasmussen et al. (this issue) take a very different perspective. The other two articles propose differing views of AMT, but such thinking is always about mathematical objects—limits, uncountable sets, groups, proportions, even proofs. In contrast, Rasmussen et al. are more concerned with how students can invent, or reinvent, for themselves at least some portions of such mathematical objects. In other words, their view of "advancing" is not so much about a student's thinking at a given time, as about the way the student develops that thinking over time and constructs some of the accompanying mathematics. Such development and construction of mathematical ideas is often encouraged when a teacher and fellow students cooperate in maintaining a classroom culture suitable for mathematizing, especially vertical mathematizing. As with Harel and Sowder's perspective, this can occur at many levels throughout a student's entire education. However, unlike the other two views on advanced mathematical thinking, it is unlikely that the topic alone, whether it be higher dimensional vector spaces or proportionality, would result in students engaging in vertical mathematizing, that is, in their advancing.

To draw a metaphor from linear algebra, the three perspectives in the following three articles move the discussion of advanced mathematical thinking forward in independent ways—ways that we hope will inspire much more work.

REFERENCES

Arcavi, A., Kessel, C., Meira, L., & Smith, J. P., III. (1998). Teaching mathematical problem solving: An analysis of an emergent classroom community. In A. H. Schoenfeld, J. Kaput, & E. Dubinsky (Eds.), *Research in collegiate mathematics education. III* (CBMS Issues in Mathematical Education, Vol. 7, pp. 1–70). Providence, RI: American Mathematical Society.

Ball, D. L. (2003). *Mathematical proficiency for all students: Toward a strategic research and development program in mathematics education* (RAND Mathematics Study Panel Report No. MR–1643.0–OERI). Santa Monica, CA: RAND Corporation.

Dahlberg, R. P., & Housman, D. L. (1997). Facilitating learning events through example generation. *Educational Studies in Mathematics, 33*, 283–299.

Dorier, J.-L. (1995). Meta level in the teaching of unifying and generalizing concepts in mathematics. *Educational Studies in Mathematics, 29*, 175–197.

Dreyfus, T. (1990). Advanced mathematical thinking. In P. Nesher & J. Kilpatrick (Eds.), *Mathematics and cognition: A research synthesis by the International Group for the Psychology of Mathematics Education* (pp. 113–134). Cambridge, UK: Cambridge University Press.

Dreyfus, T. (Ed.). (1995). Advanced mathematical thinking [Special issue]. *Educational Studies in Mathematics, 29*(2).

Dubinsky, E. (Ed.). (1997). An investigation of students' understanding of abstract algebra (binary operations, groups and subgroups) and the use of abstract structures to build other structures (through cosets, normality and quotient groups) [Special issue]. *The Journal of Mathematical Behavior, 16*(3).

Edwards, B. (1997). An undergraduate student's understanding and use of mathematical definitions in real analysis. In J. A. Dossey, J. O. Swafford, M. Parmantie, & A. E. Dossey (Eds.), *Proceedings of the 19th Annual Meeting of the North American Chapter of the International Group for the Psychology of Mathematics Education* (Vol. 1, pp. 17–22). Columbus, OH: The ERIC Clearinghouse for Science, Mathematics, and Environmental Education.

Edwards, B. S., Dubinsky, E., & McDonald, M. A. (2005). Advanced mathematical thinking. *Mathematical Thinking and Learning, 7,* 15–25.

Edwards, B. S., & Ward, M. B. (2004). Surprises from mathematics education research: Student (mis)use of mathematical definitions. *The American Mathematical Monthly, 111*(5), 411–424.

Hadamard, J. (1945). *The psychology of invention in the mathematical field.* Princeton, NJ: Princeton University Press.

Harel, G., & Sowder, L. (2005). Advanced mathematical-thinking at any age: Its nature and its development. *Mathematical Thinking and Learning, 7,* 27–50.

Heid, M. K., Ferrini-Mundy, J., Graham, K., & Harel, G. (1998). The role of advanced mathematical thinking in mathematics education reform. In S. Berenson, K. Dawkins, M. Blanton, W. Coulombe, J. Kolb, K. Norwood, & L. Stiff (Eds.), *Proceedings of the 20th Annual Meeting of the North American Chapter of the International Group for the Psychology of Mathematics Education* (Vol. 1, pp. 53–58). Columbus, OH: ERIC Clearinghouse for Science, Mathematics, and Environmental Education.

Heid, M. K., Ferrini-Mundy, J., Graham, K., Harel, G., Edwards, B., Ivey, K., et al. (1999). The role of advanced mathematical thinking in mathematics education reform. In F. Hitt & M. Santos (Eds.), *Proceedings of the 21st Annual Meeting of the North American Chapter of the International Group for the Psychology of Mathematics Education* (Vol. 1, pp. 164–169). Columbus, OH: ERIC Clearinghouse for Science, Mathematics, and Environmental Education.

Heid, M. K., Harel, G., Ferrini-Mundy, J., & Graham, K. (2000). Advanced mathematical thinking: Implications of various perspective on advanced mathematical thinking for mathematics education reform. In M. L. Fernández (Ed.), *Proceedings of the 22nd Annual Meeting of the North American Chapter of the International Group for the Psychology of Mathematics Education* (Vol. 1, pp. 33–37). Columbus, OH: ERIC Clearinghouse for Science, Mathematics, and Environmental Education.

Lakatos, I. (1976). *Proofs and refutations: The logic of mathematical discovery.* Cambridge, UK: Cambridge University Press.

Leron, U., Hazzan, O., & Zazkis, R. (1995). Learning group isomorphism: A crossroads of many concepts. *Educational Studies in Mathematics, 29,* 153–174.

Lobato, J., & Siebert, D. (2002). Quantitative reasoning in a reconceived view of transfer. *The Journal of Mathematical Behavior, 21,* 87–116.

Maher, C. A., & Martino, A. M. (1996a). The development of the idea of proof. A five-year case study. *Journal for Research in Mathematics Education, 27,* 194–219.

Maher, C. A., & Martino, A. M. (1996b). Young children invent methods of proof: The "Gang of Four." In L. Steffe, P. Nesher, P. Cobb, G. Goldin, & B. Greer (Eds.), *Theories of mathematical learning* (pp. 431–447). Mahwah, NJ: Lawrence Erlbaum Associates, Inc.

Maher, C. A., & Martino, A. M. (1997). Conditions for conceptual change: From pattern recognition to theory posting. In H. Mansfield & N. A. Pateman (Eds.), *Young children and mathematics: Concepts and their representation.* Sydney, Australia: Australian Association of Mathematics Teachers.

Maher, C. A., & Speiser, R. (1997). How far can you go with a tower of blocks? In E. Pehkonen (Ed.), *Proceedings of the 21st Conference of the International Group for the Psychology of Mathematics Education* (Vol. 4, pp. 174–183). Jyväskylä, Finland: Gummerus.

National Council of Teachers of Mathematics (NCTM). (2000). *Principles and standards for school mathematics*. Reston, VA: The National Council of Teachers of Mathematics.

Nesher, P., & Kilpatrick, J. (Eds.). (1990). *Mathematics and cognition: A research synthesis by the International Group for the Psychology of Mathematics Education*. Cambridge, UK: Cambridge University Press.

Pimm, D. (1995). The advance party. [Review of the book *Advanced mathematical thinking*]. *Educational Studies in Mathematics, 29*, 97–122.

Rasmussen, C., Zandieh, M. (2000). Defining as a mathematical activity: A realistic mathematics analysis. In M. L. Fernández (Ed.), *Proceedings of the 22nd Annual Meeting of the North American Chapter of the International Group for the Psychology of Mathematics Education* (Vol. 1, pp. 301–305). Columbus, OH: The ERIC Clearinghouse for Science, Mathematics, and Environmental Education.

Rasmussen, C., & Zandieh, M., King, K., & Teppo, A. (2005). Advancing mathematical activity: A practice-oriented view of advanced mathematical thinking. *Mathematical Thinking and Learning, 7*, 51–73.

Resnick, L. B., Nesher, P., Leonard, F., Magone, M., Omanson, S., & Peled, I. (1989). Conceptual bases of arithmetic errors: The case of decimal fractions. *Journal for Research in Mathematics Education, 20*, 8–27.

Schoenfeld, A. H. (1985). *Mathematical problem solving*. Orlando, FL: Academic Press.

Selden, A., & Selden, J. (2003). Validations of proofs considered as texts: Can undergraduates tell whether an argument proves a theorem? *Journal for Research in Mathematics Education, 34*, 4–36.

Sierpinska, A., Defence, A., Khatcherian, T., & Saldanha, L. (1997). A propos de trois modes de raisonnement en algèbre linéaire [Three modes of reasoning in linear algebra]. In J.-L. Dorier (Ed.), *L'enseignement de l'algèbre linéaire en question* (pp. 259–268). Grenoble, France: La Pensée Sauvage.

Tall, D. (Ed.). (1991). *Advanced mathematical thinking*. Dordrecht, The Netherlands: Kluwer Academic.

Tall, D. (1995). Cognitive growth in elementary and advanced mathematical thinking. In L. Meira & D. Carraher (Eds.), *Proceedings of the 19th International Conference for the Psychology of Mathematics Education* (Vol. 1, pp. 61–75). Recife, Brazil: Universidade Federal de Pernambuco.

Thompson, P. W. (1993). Yes, Virginia, some children do grow up to be mathematicians. [Review of the book *Advanced mathematical thinking*]. *Journal for Research in Mathematics Education, 24*, 279–284.

Thurston, W. P. (1994). On proof and progress in mathematics. *Bulletin of the AMS, 30*, 161–177.

Treffers, A. (1987). *Three dimensions. A model of goal and theory description in mathematics education: The Wiskobas project*. Dordrecht, The Netherlands: Kluwer Academic.

MATHEMATICAL THINKING AND LEARNING, 7(1), 15–25

Advanced Mathematical Thinking

Barbara S. Edwards
Department of Mathematics
Oregon State University

Ed Dubinsky
Department of Mathematical Sciences
Kent State University

Michael A. McDonald
Department of Mathematics
Occidental College

In this article we propose the following definition for *advanced mathematical thinking*: Thinking that requires deductive and rigorous reasoning about mathematical notions that are not entirely accessible to us through our five senses. We argue that this definition is not necessarily tied to a particular kind of educational experience; nor is it tied to a particular level of mathematics. We also give examples to illustrate the distinction we make between advanced mathematical thinking and *elementary mathematical thinking*. In particular, we discuss which kind of thinking may be required depending on the size of a mathematical problem, including problems involving infinity, and the types of models that are available.

Over the past two decades, the study of "advanced mathematical thinking" has attracted increased interest, even though there is little agreement on what is meant by "advanced mathematical thinking." A broad definition of advanced mathematical thinking (AMT) might include thinking that seems to be "advanced" for one's age or grade level. By this definition, very young students who offer insightful comments or work that seems to be beyond the ability of most children their age could be said to be employing AMT. For example, the often-repeated story about young Carl Friederich Gauss, who surprised his teacher when he quickly summed the first

Requests for reprints should be sent to Barbara S. Edwards, Department of Mathematics, Kidder Hall 368, Oregon State University, Corvallis, OR 97331–4605. E-mail: edwards@math.oregonstate.edu

100 positive integers by inventing an algorithm, would certainly represent "advanced" thinking for a child his age. At the other extreme, one might more narrowly define advanced mathematical thinking as being associated only with cutting-edge research in mathematics.

Many mathematics educators have used the phrase "advanced mathematical thinking" as a characterization that would most often describe certain kinds of student thinking in collegiate level mathematics or some of the mathematical thinking at the professional level of mathematics. In our definition we focus on the phenomenon that seems to first occur during a mathematics student's experience in undergraduate mathematics when he or she first begins to deal with abstract concepts and deductive proof. At this time students often recognize that many of the thinking skills that contributed to their success in calculus courses no longer work in courses such as introductory real analysis or abstract algebra.

The purpose of this article is to define advanced mathematical thinking in a way that loosely links AMT to this transitional period in a mathematics student's education. We illustrate our definition with examples of mathematical situations, contrasting what we think of as advanced mathematical thinking with more elementary mathematical thinking (EMT).

EARLIER DEFINITIONS OF ADVANCED
MATHEMATICAL THINKING

In the following statement, Robert and Schwarzenberger (1991) described learning in advanced mathematics courses as different from learning in elementary mathematics courses:

> There is a quantitative change [from elementary mathematics to advanced mathematics]: more concepts, less time, the need for greater powers of reflection, greater abstraction, fewer meaningful problems, more emphasis on proof, greater need for versatile learning, greater need for personal control over learning. The confusion caused by new definitions coincides with the need for more abstract deductive thought. Taken together these quantitative changes engender a qualitative change, that characterizes the transition to advanced mathematical thinking. (p. 133)

It is unclear in their statement how much of the difference they noted is due to pedagogical and curricular issues that are traditionally associated with college-level teaching rather than to the mathematics itself. Furthermore, to some degree, some of the changes described above occur throughout one's learning experience in mathematics. For instance, the transition in middle school from arithmetic to algebra could be said to involve the need for greater powers of reflection, greater abstraction, and fewer meaningful problems.

Tall (1992) linked his notion of advanced mathematical thinking to formal mathematics. He characterized AMT as consisting of "two important components: precise mathematical definition (including the statement of axioms in axiomatic theories) and logical deductions of theorems based upon them." He went on to say,

> The move to more advanced mathematical thinking involves a difficult transition, from a position where concepts have an intuitive basis founded on experience to one where they are specified by formal definitions and their properties reconstructed through logical deductions. (Tall, 1992, p. 495)

We propose a definition that directly addresses the "thinking." Although it is true that advanced mathematics students and professional mathematicians work with concepts that are "specified by formal definitions and their properties reconstructed through logical deduction" (Tall, 1992, p. 495), the thinking that is required is not always what we define as advanced mathematical thinking. Edwards (1997, 1999) found that students could often successfully (and perhaps superficially) reason from formal definitions if these definitions did not conflict with their previous mathematical understandings and experiences. The difficulties for some students began when they were reasoning about concepts that were not physically accessible to them and their intuitions and the definitions conflicted.

Edwards (1997) gave an example of a student called Stephanie, who at one point was asked to complete some tasks using the following definition for infinite decimal.

Definition. Let $c_1, c_2, ..., c_n, ...$ be an infinite sequence of integers with $0 \le c_i \le 9$. The number, $\sup\{ .c_1 c_2 ...c_n ; n = 1,2,3,...\}$ is denoted by $.c_1 c_2 ...c_n...$ and is called an infinite decimal.

First, Stephanie addressed the possible equivalence of .333... and 1/3. She successfully argued that 1/3 equals sup $\{.3, .33, .333, ...\}$ because it is the smallest possible upper bound for the sequence; thus, 1/3 must equal .333.... But when faced with the possible equivalence of .999... and 1, she said that this one was not possible. She explained that it was clear that 1/3 and .333... are the same number because when you divide 3 into 1 you get .333..., but "if you divide 1 into 1 you don't get .999...!" (Edwards, 1997, p. 20). It is clear that Stephanie was not really reasoning from the definition, but instead from her earlier experience of changing a fractional representation to a decimal representation by dividing the numerator by the denominator. Her intuitions collided with her understanding of the mathematical definitions and her intuitions prevailed.

DEFINING ADVANCED MATHEMATICAL THINKING

Our definition of AMT shares some characteristics of earlier definitions. We propose to define advanced mathematical thinking as follows: Advanced mathematical thinking is thinking that requires deductive and rigorous reasoning about mathematical notions that are not entirely accessible to us through our five senses.[1] Our definition has close connections with what Saunders Mac Lane (1981) wrote concerning the source of mathematics. Mac Lane stated that mathematics comes from the application of logic and rigor to human activities. For example, he said that counting is the source of arithmetic and number theory; and estimating is the source of probability, measure theory, and statistics. Mac Lane, however, did not differentiate between activities that can be accomplished with the use of the five senses and those that cannot. Thus, he did not set up the categorization of elementary mathematical thinking and advanced mathematical thinking.

Although the impetus for creating our definition was prompted by our observations of students undergoing the transition from calculus to more advanced mathematics courses, it is not necessarily tied to a particular kind of educational experience; nor is it tied to a particular educational level of mathematics. We do not claim that there is some point in one's educational experience (or in one's mathematical career) when elementary mathematical thinking ends and advanced mathematical thinking begins. In our view, AMT resides on a continuum of mathematical thought that seems to transcend, but does not ignore, the procedural experiences or intuitions of elementary mathematical thinking.

Both conditions—the deductive and rigorous reasoning and the inaccessibility of the mathematical notions to our senses—are necessary in order for thinking to be considered AMT. While the limit in real analysis is a notion whose full understanding requires deductive and rigorous reasoning about an inaccessible process, we could not claim that all thinking about limits is advanced. In calculus courses students are often required to evaluate limits, however this activity does not necessarily require advanced mathematical thinking because it can often be reduced to an automated symbolic manipulation. On the other hand, deductive and rigorous reasoning is required of students in high school geometry, however the ideas, or the representations of the ideas, about which the students are asked to reason in the context of high school geometry are usually accessible to them through examples in the physical world. Thus the important characteristic of our definition of advanced mathematical thinking is the combination of the need for deductive and rigorous reasoning about concepts and the fact that these concepts are not accessible to the individual through the five senses.

It is important to note that we recognize that the use of the word *advanced* is problematic. We may seem to imply that thinking that is not AMT is somehow inferior, and that is not our intent. However, to remain consistent with earlier literature we continue to use the phrase.

---

[1]We refer to the conventional five senses of hearing, sight, touch, taste, and smell. Some are probably more applicable than others.

In what follows we hope to make clear the distinction we see between elementary mathematical thinking and advanced mathematical thinking and to ask and answer questions that are related to our definition.

SIZE OF THE PROBLEM

There are many mathematical questions that when posed one way might only require EMT, but when posed in a different way would require AMT. Consider, for example, the following question.

> Given an m by n rectangle, where m and n are integer inches, tiled by one-inch squares, how many tiles must the diagonal of the rectangle intersect?

A student can solve this problem by carefully constructing models of rectangles of different measure and looking for a pattern in the answers for each example. The student may realize that the examples divide into two equivalence classes, depending upon whether or not m and n are relatively prime. He or she can then create a general formula for solving this problem for any integer values of m and n. By our definition this activity would involve EMT because actual paper and pencil models can be created to assist the problem solver.

Suppose, however, that the question were written as follows.

> Given a rectangular parallelepiped measured in inches as a by b by c, where a, b, and c are integers, and sectioned by one-inch cubes, how many cubes must be intersected by the diagonal line that connects the front lower left corner to the back upper right corner?

Thinking about this new problem is more complex, however because it is still possible to create a model and to reason from particular examples, the thinking required to solve this problem would still not be considered AMT by our definition. Could we say that thinking about this problem without a model would be AMT? Possibly, but a more definitive situation would be to extend the problem into multidimensional space where one would have to reason from examples and models in lower dimensional spaces. Any models in the higher dimensions would be purely mental and not accessible to the five senses.

In some sense it seems that the "size" of the problem in this example is an important factor in determining whether or not a successful solution requires AMT. Once this problem goes beyond three dimensions it is no longer directly accessible to our senses and although one may reason from the lower dimensional situations, one must eventually reason in higher dimensions to attack the problem. We propose then that size could be a determining factor in deciding what is accessible to our five senses and thus which situation would require EMT and which would require AMT. For this problem, three dimensions or fewer would require only EMT, but greater than three dimensions might require AMT.

We cannot say, however, that reasoning about any figure that has three or fewer dimensions would never require AMT. In *What is Mathematics?* (1941) Courant and Robbins have depicted a simple, closed curve that is so twisty, it is impossible using only one's senses to tell whether a given point is inside or outside the region bounded by the curve. Using AMT, however, one could understand that following a straight line from the given point one need merely count the intersections with the curve in moving to a region that is clearly outside.

PROBLEMS INVOLVING INFINITY

Problems involving infinity—either infinite processes or objects with infinite cardinality—also contain this aspect of size. We suggest that considering the countably infinite natural numbers may not require AMT, but comparing $|\mathbf{N}|$ with $|2\mathbf{N}|$ may require AMT. The ability to understand that there is a one-to-one relationship between $\mathbf{N}$ and $2\mathbf{N}$ is probably not available through experience in the physical world. In their article, Brown, McDonald, and Weller (2009) proposed a theoretical description of how a student might construct an understanding of infinite iterative processes such as might define the explicit one-to-one correspondence between these two sets. While the construction is based on finite iterative processes of producing one object from a prior object, at some point the individual must realize that this iterative process holds for all of the infinite objects. This requires the individual to see the infinite process as being complete, even though there is no final step, and no final object is obtained. We argue that this, in and of itself, may not require AMT. It is the ability to transcend this process and reason accurately about the entirety of the process and what is obtained from the completion of the process that exemplifies AMT. We illustrate this in the following.

In their article, Brown et al. (2004) examined students' reasoning about whether or not the following equality holds.

$$\cup_{k=1}^{\infty} P(\{1, 2, \ldots, k\}) = P(N),$$

where P denotes the power set of the given set and N is the set of natural numbers. A student they called Emily could conceive of the infinite union as being complete, even though she obviously could not access it explicitly through physical models. However, she was still unable to rigorously prove whether the equality held or not. In particular, with respect to the infinite union, Emily said that "if you infinitely union sets, eventually you've got to union the infinite set I would think.... When do you ever reach infinity?" Ultimately she was not able to show that the equality does not hold, unlike the student described in the following section.

The next step in the construction proposed by Brown et al. (2004) clearly requires AMT. Trying to find the parallel to finite processes, the individual feels pressure to ask a question such as "What does one have when this process is complete?" This requires the individual to see the completed process as a totality, that is, all infinite objects are present in the individual's mind at a moment in time. This attempted action of asking such a question may lead the individual to encapsulate the process into a cognitive object,[2] thus creating what Brown et al. call a "transcendent object" that he or she places in relation to the completed infinite iterative sequence. This transcendent object is outside of the process and is not produced by the process; it is the product of the encapsulation of the process. The student referred to as Tobi in Brown et al. understood the nature of all of the steps of the infinite union, and understood the nature of the transcendent object. Ultimately, she was able to state that the left hand side "is the union of an infinite number of finite sets." We believe she was engaged in AMT because she not only conceived of the infinite process as complete, something clearly not accessible to her through any physical model, but she also rigorously reasoned about the nature of the sets present in the transcendent object of the process and how this object compared with another object, namely P(N).

Likewise by our definition, deductive and rigorous reasoning about the infinite process involved in the concept of limit requires AMT, even though we often see students talking about limits without using AMT. In dealing with limits, students often struggle with the human need to make sense of things by attempting to carry out a process that is impossible to see to the end. Students who view the concept of limit as a dynamic process (meaning a process of getting closer and closer to a limit, but not the object that is the limit) or an unreachable bound, for example, are demonstrating in this instance a failure to use AMT as they are not transcending the finite physical models available to them.

For example, a student trying to reason about

$$\lim_{x \to 1} \frac{x-1}{x^2-1}$$

might plug in x = 1.1, then x = 1.01, then x = 1.001, and so on and get a sense that the limit appears to be approaching the value ½. The student may even say that the limit is ½, but this still does not demonstrate a use of AMT. Rather an individual is engaged in AMT if he or she sees the limit as a coordinated pair of processes, the domain process of approaching 1 and the range process of approaching ½, coordinated by the function (Cottrill et al., 1996). In addition, he or she should see that

---

[2] Even though a student may try to perform the action on the process, he or she may not actually succeed in encapsulating the process into an object. The attempt at performing an action on a process spurs a student to encapsulation, but it may not be enough to guarantee encapsulation.

these processes can be completed even though no last step is reached and no last object is produced, see the processes as totalities, and ultimately see that the limit is the transcendent object associated with the encapsulation of the range process (i.e., the limit is exactly equal to ½ even though ½ is never actually produced by the process).

RIGOROUS AND DEDUCTIVE REASONING

We have said that to qualify as AMT, one's reasoning must be rigorous and deductive. Certainly careful deductive reasoning is also rigorous but we believe that requiring strictly deductive reasoning would be too limiting. When is reasoning rigorous enough to qualify for the label of AMT?

This leads to an interesting question. Was Isaac Newton using advanced mathematical thinking when he invented calculus? Bishop Berkeley's characterization of Newton's "ghosts of departed quantities" suggests that at least he found Newton's rigor lacking in what Berkeley saw as a seemingly casual use of infinitesimals (cf. Boyer, 1985). To be sure, the definition of limit that we use today was unavailable to Newton (although he came very close to it[3]) and the language Newton used to describe his ideas was awkward even for his time, but his ideas were developed in a rigorous way. He developed a rigorous method of analyzing infinite series and in the invention of calculus applied this method of analysis to the age-old problems of finding rates of change and areas under curves.

Newton's Binomial Method linked the operations on finite polynomial expressions to those on infinite series. Although Pascal had already developed a method for finding the coefficients in a binomial expansion of $(a + b)^n$, where n equals a positive integer (using what is now known as Pascal's Triangle), it was Newton who developed a generalized formula applicable to binomial expansions where n is any positive or negative rational number. Pascal's method could deal with binomials such as $(a + b)^3$, that when expanded terminates after four terms. Newton's method could deal with the expansion of expressions such as $(a + b)^{-3}$ and $(a + b)^{1/3}$ for which the series expression on the right hand side of the equation never terminates. Newton was able to reason about these infinite series using a finite series model and to prove that his formulas worked. He then combined his binomial theorem with his method of *fluxions* to build differential and integral calculus. The creation of accessible models to represent seemingly inaccessible concepts plays an important role in AMT. The following example illustrates the complexity involved in using "imperfect" models.

---

[3]In Newton's treatise *Philosophiae Naturalis Principia*, he writes of "Quantities, and the ratios of quantities, that in any finite time converge continually to equality, and before the end of that time approach nearer to each other than by any given difference, become ultimately equal" (Boyer, 1985, p. 436).

THE USE OF MODELS

In mathematics when one reasons about objects that are not accessible to the five senses, it is often necessary to create models that depict one or more, but not all, of the characteristics of the desired object. There are, for instance, "imperfect" models that attempt to depict the Klein bottle in this way. The mathematician uses these models to assist in creating a mental model that becomes real to her or him. Since these mental models cannot be directly communicated to others, there are potential difficulties especially when designing models for use in the teaching of mathematics.

In a recent course taught by one of the authors, students were engaged in reasoning about familiar geometric shapes such as triangles and straight lines in Euclidean, spherical, and hyperbolic spaces. For the most part, the models that the students used to represent Euclidean and spherical space accurately depicted the represented spaces. The models for the hyperbolic plane were created by crocheting an object in which the number of stitches from one row to the next was increased by a constant ratio of 5:6 (see Henderson, 2001, pp. 49–51). The resulting objects resembled ballerinas' tutus (see Figure 1) and were necessarily "imperfect" representations of the hyperbolic plane.

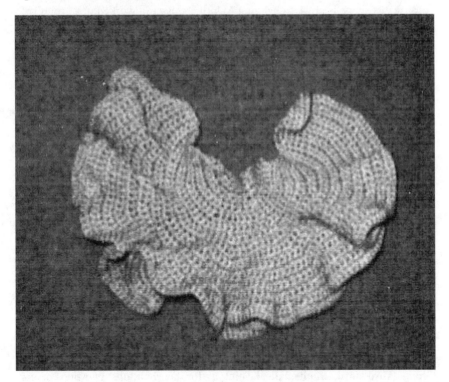

FIGURE 1   Crocheted model of hyperbolic plane.

The instructor's intent was that these models would assist students in creating better mental models from which to reason. This was no easy task, but many students experienced some level of success over the duration of the course. For example, a student called Tia, talked about how she used the model in an interview following the completion of the course. Tia said,

> I knew that the [crocheted model] wasn't exactly hyperbolic space, but I had to just use it to find out what a straight line would be and from there I thought about what hyperbolic space in my head… sort of based on what I saw in [the model]…. I tried to find the logical conclusion of what things would have to be true if these were the straight lines.

We claim Tia was employing AMT in her use of the crocheted model for hyperbolic space.

Another student, called Jim, however, was not able to see beyond the actual model. Jim seemed grounded by elementary mathematical thinking. He talked about the "wobbly" and "stretchy" nature of the hyperbolic plane and at one point he wrote on an exam that there were no "real" symmetries on the hyperbolic plane because "its shape is always changing." During class Jim worked in a group with another student (we will call him Mark) who seemed to have produced a sufficient mental model of the hyperbolic plane. Mark tried many times to share his mental model with Jim, but because it was only real for Mark and not accessible to Jim through his senses, Jim was not able to benefit from it.

CONCLUSION

Exemplary mathematical thinking may occur at any age of student and level of mathematics, but the particular notion that we describe as advanced mathematical thinking occurs only under certain conditions involving rigorous and deductive reasoning about mathematical objects that are unavailable to our five senses. This definition can help mathematics educators focus on the difficult transition period as students move from calculus to more abstract and theoretical courses in mathematics. In our view it embodies the essence of the difficulty that students experience.

ACKNOWLEDGMENTS

The authors thank the many people who participated in the PME–NA Working Group on Advanced Mathematical Thinking for their helpful suggestions on earlier versions of this article. We also thank the reviewers who gave us many helpful suggestions during the various stages of development of this article.

REFERENCES

Boyer, C. B. (1985). *A history of mathematics.* Princeton, NJ: Princeton University Press.

Brown, A., McDonald, M. A., & Weller, K. (2004). *Students' conceptions of infinite iterative processes.* Manuscript submitted.

Cottrill, J., Dubinsky, E., Nichols, D., Schwingendorf, K., Thomas, K., & Vidakovic, D. (1996). Understanding the limit concept: Beginning with a coordinated process schema. *Journal of Mathematical Behavior, 15,* 167–192.

Courant, R., & Robbins H. (1941). *What is mathematics? An elementary approach to ideas and methods.* London: Oxford University Press.

Edwards, B. (1997). An undergraduate student's understanding and use of mathematical definitions in real analysis. In J. A. Dossey, J. O. Swafford, M. Parmantie, & A. E. Dossey (Eds.), *Proceedings of the 19th Annual Meeting of the North American Chapter of the International Group for the Psychology of Mathematics Education* (Vol. 1, pp. 17–22). Columbus, OH: The ERIC Clearinghouse for Science, Mathematics, and Environmental Education.

Edwards, B. (1999). Revising the notion of concept image/concept definition. In F. Hitt & M. Santos (Eds.), *Proceedings of the 21st Annual Meeting of the North American Chapter of the International Group for the Psychology of Mathematics Education* (Vol. 2, pp. 205–210). Columbus, OH: The ERIC Clearinghouse for Science, Mathematics, and Environmental Education.

Henderson, D. W. (2001). *Experiencing geometry* (2nd ed.). Upper Saddle River, NJ: Prentice Hall.

Mac Lane, S. (1981). Mathematical models: A sketch for the philosophy of mathematics. *The American Mathematical Monthly, 88,* 462–472.

Robert, A., & Schwarzenberger, R. (1991). Research in teaching and learning mathematics at an advanced level. In D. Tall (Ed.), *Advanced mathematical thinking* (pp. 127–139). Dordrecht, The Netherlands: Kluwer Academic.

Tall, D. (1992). The transition to advanced mathematical thinking: Functions, limits, infinity and proof. In D. A. Grouws (Ed.), *NCTM handbook of research on mathematics teaching and learning* (pp. 495–511). New York: Macmillan.

MATHEMATICAL THINKING AND LEARNING, 7(1), 27–50

Advanced Mathematical-Thinking at Any Age: Its Nature and Its Development

Guershon Harel
Department of Mathematics
University of California, San Diego

Larry Sowder
Department of Mathematics and Statistics
San Diego State University

This article argues that *advanced mathematical thinking*, usually conceived as thinking in advanced mathematics, might profitably be viewed as advanced thinking in mathematics (*advanced mathematical-thinking*). Hence, advanced mathematical-thinking can properly be viewed as potentially starting in elementary school. The definition of mathematical thinking entails considering the epistemological and didactical obstacles to a particular way of thinking. The interplay between ways of thinking and ways of understanding gives a contrast between the two, to make clearer the broader view of mathematical thinking and to suggest implications for instructional practices. The latter are summarized with a description of the DNR system (Duality, Necessity, and Repeated Reasoning). Certain common assumptions about instruction are criticized (in an effort to be provocative) by suggesting that they can interfere with growth in mathematical thinking.

The reader may have noticed the unusual location of the hyphen in the title of this article. We relocated the hyphen in "advanced-mathematical thinking" (i.e., thinking in advanced mathematics) so that the phrase reads, "advanced mathematical-thinking" (i.e., mathematical thinking of an advanced nature). This change in emphasis is to argue that a student's growth in mathematical thinking is an evolving process, and that the nature of mathematical thinking should be studied so as to

---

Requests for reprints should be sent to Guershon Harel, Department of Mathematics, University of California, San Diego, San Diego, CA 92093–0112. E-mail: harel@math.ucsd.edu

lead to coherent instruction aimed toward advanced mathematical-thinking. These arguments are embodied in our responses to four questions:

1. What is meant by "mathematical thinking"?[1]
2. What are the characteristics of advanced mathematical-thinking?
3. What are concrete reasoning practices by which advanced mathematical-thinking can be enhanced?
4. What are concrete reasoning practices by which advanced mathematical-thinking can be hindered?

We address these questions, in turn, in the four sections comprising this article.

Our earlier research necessitated these questions in the context of mathematical proof (cf. Harel, 2001; Harel & Sowder, 1998). In this article, however, we do not restrict our discussion to the process of proving. Rather, we demonstrate our claims in a range of mathematical contexts across the grade-level spectrum, to demonstrate that advanced mathematical-thinking is not bound by advanced-mathematical thinking.

ARTICLE'S ORGANIZATION

This article is organized in three sections (followed by a brief conclusion section):

1. Our definition of advanced mathematical thinking is based on an important distinction between two categories of knowledge: *ways of understanding* and *ways of thinking*. In the first section, we define these notions and discuss several responses and solutions by students to illustrate them. In particular, we show how "proof schemes" (what constitutes truth for an individual), "problem-solving approaches," and "beliefs about mathematics" are instances of one's ways of thinking.

2. Our definition of advanced mathematical thinking also utilizes Brousseau's (1997) notion of *epistemological obstacle*. Therefore, in the second section, we discuss this important notion to argue for our relativistic view of the property "advanced" and to discuss examples of epistemological obstacles involved in the development of advanced mathematical thinking (relative to our definition).

3. Finally, in the third section, we point to general reasoning practices by which advanced mathematical thinking can be advanced or hindered.

---

[1]We use the terms *mathematical thinking, a way of mathematical thinking,* or just *a way of thinking* interchangeably, although we are always referring to a mathematical context.

WHAT IS MEANT BY "MATHEMATICAL THINKING"?

Underlying the analysis presented in this article is the fundamental premise that humans' mental actions, observable or inferred, are induced and governed by their general views of the world, and, conversely, humans' general views of the world are formed by these actions. Our probe into the above four questions through the lenses of this duality led to a distinction between two categories of knowledge: ways of thinking and ways of understanding.

The particular meaning students give to a term, sentence, or text, the solution they provide to a problem, or the justification they use to validate or refute an assertion—are ways of understanding, whereas students' general theories—implicit or explicit—underlying such actions are ways of thinking. This distinction, to be elaborated upon shortly, has been both essential and valuable for our research and for its instructional implications. We have observed that teachers often form, at least implicitly, cognitive objectives in terms of ways of thinking, but their efforts to these teach ways of thinking are often counterproductive because their efforts do not build on ways of understanding. Conversely, teachers often focus on ways of understanding but overlook the goal of helping students construct effective ways of thinking from these ways of understanding. This observation is the basis for the Duality Principle, one of the fundamental principles that underlie the instructional treatment employed in our teaching experiments (see Harel, 1998, 2001). We return to the Duality Principle in the third section of this article.

WAYS OF THINKING VERSUS WAYS OF UNDERSTANDING

We describe the distinction between ways of thinking and ways of understanding in the context in which it initially arose. Consider the following three central, often interrelated, mathematical activities:

1. Comprehension of mathematical content, as when reading texts or listening to others.
2. Carrying out an investigation, as when solving a problem.
3. Establishing truth, as when justifying or refuting.

Although it is pedagogically useful to distinguish among the three activities, cognitively they can easily be subsumed under item (2), problem solving; for comprehension and communication, as well as justifying or proving, are all problem-solving processes.

Corresponding to these three types of mathematical activities, the phrase, ways of understanding, refers to

1. The particular meaning/interpretation a person gives to a concept, relationships between concepts, assertions, or problems.
2. The particular solution a person provides to a problem.
3. The particular evidence a person offers to establish or refute a mathematical assertion.

Examples of ways of understanding for (1) include the following: A student may read or say the words, "derivative of a function," understanding the phrase as meaning the slope of a line tangent to the graph of a function, as the best linear approximation to a function near a point, as a rate of change, etc. On the other hand, a student may understand this concept superficially (e.g., "the derivative is nx^{n-1} for x^n") or incorrectly (e.g., "the derivative is the quotient $(f(x + h) - f(x))/h$"). Similarly, a student may understand the concept of a fraction in different ways. For example, the student may understand the symbol a/b in terms of *unit fraction* (a/b is a $1/b$ units); in terms of *part-whole* (a/b is a units out of b units); in terms of *partitive division* (a/b is the quantity that results from a units being divided equally into b parts); in terms of *quotitive division* (a/b is the measure of a in terms of b-units). All of these would be ways of understanding derivatives or ways of understanding fractions.

Examples of ways of understanding for (2)—particular methods of solving a problem—can be seen in the following. A ninth-grade class was assigned the following problem:

Problem 1: A pool is connected to 2 pipes. One pipe can fill the pool in 20 hours, and the other in 30 hours. Assuming the water is flowing at a constant rate, how long will it take the 2 pipes together to fill the pool?

Among the different solutions provided by the students, there were the following four—each represents a different way of understanding.

Solution 1.1: In 12 hours the first pipe would fill 3/5 of the pool and the second pipe the remaining 2/5. (The student who provided this solution accompanied it with a sketch similar to Figure 1. We return to this solution later in the article).

Solution 1.2: It will take the 2 pipes 50 hours to fill the pool.

Solution 1.3: It will take the 2 pipes 10 hours to fill the pool.

Solution 1.4: It would take x hours. In one hour the first pipe will fill 1/20 of the pool, whereas the second will fill 1/30. In x hours the first pipe would fill

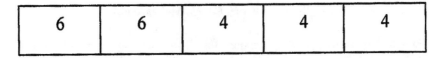

6	6	4	4	4

FIGURE 1   Student's sketch for Solution 1.1.

$x/20$ and the second, $x/30$. Thus, $x/20 + x/30 = 1$. (The student then solved this equation to obtain $x = 12$.)

Examples of ways of understanding for (3)—justifying or refuting—include the following justifications by prospective secondary teachers to the problem:

Problem 2: Prove that $\log(a_1 \cdot a_2 \ldots a_n) = \log a_1 + \log a_2 + \ldots + \log a_n$ for all positive integers n.

Solution 2.1:
  $\log(4 \cdot 3 \cdot 7) = \log 84 = 1.924$
  $\log 4 + \log 3 + \log 7 = 1.924$
  $\log(4 \cdot 3 \cdot 6) = \log 72 = 1.857$
  $\log 4 + \log 3 + \log 6 = 1.857$
  Because these work, then $\log(a_1 \cdot a_2 \ldots a_n) = \log a_1 + \log a_2 + \ldots + \log a_n$.

Solution 2.2:
  i. $\log(a_1 a_2) = \log a_1 + \log a_2$ by definition
     $\log(a_1 a_2 a_3) = \log a_1 + \log a_2 a_3$. Similar to $\log(ax)$ as in step (i), where this time $x = a_2 a_3$.

  Then

  ii. $\log(a_1 a_2 a_3) = \log a_1 + \log a_2 + \log a_3$
     We can see from step (ii) any $\log(a_1 a_2 a_3 \ldots a_n)$ can be repeatedly broken down to $\log a_1 + \log a_2 + \log a_n$.

In our usage, the phrase way of understanding, conveys the reasoning one applies in a local, particular mathematical situation. The phrase way of thinking, on the other hand, refers to what governs one's ways of understanding, and thus expresses reasoning that is not specific to one particular situation but to a multitude of situations. A person's ways of thinking involve at least three interrelated categories: beliefs, problem-solving approaches, and proof schemes.

BELIEFS—VIEWS OF MATHEMATICS

"Formal mathematics has little or nothing to do with real thinking or problem solving," and "The solution of a problem should not take more than five minutes" are detrimental common beliefs among students (Schoenfeld, 1985, p. 43). On the other hand, in our work with undergraduate mathematics students, we found that enabling beliefs such as "A concept can have multiple interpretations" and "It is advantageous to possess multiple interpretations of a concept," although essential in courses such as linear algebra, are often absent from the students' repertoires of reasoning. The development of these ways of thinking should not wait until students take advanced-mathematics courses, such as linear algebra. Elementary school mathematics and secondary school mathematics are rich with opportunities for students to develop these ways of thinking. For example, the different ways of understanding fractions we just presented should provide such an opportunity to develop the above ways of thinking for all elementary-grade students; likewise the (correct) different ways of understanding derivatives should provide such an opportunity for secondary-school students who take calculus.

PROBLEM-SOLVING APPROACHES[2]

"Look for a simpler problem," "Consider alternative possibilities while attempting to solve a problem," "Look for a key word in the problem statement" are examples of problem-solving approaches. The latter way of thinking might have governed the way of understanding expressed in Solution 1.2. Which ways of thinking might have governed the other three solutions to Problem 1? Of particular interest is Solution 1.1. Only one student, G, provided this solution, and she was briefly interviewed. G indicated that she drew a diagram—a rectangle to represent the pool (Figure 1)—and divided it into 5 equal parts. Then she noticed that 3(20/5) is the same as 2(30/5). G was unwilling (or unable) to answer the question of how she thought to divide the rectangle into 5 equal parts, so we can only conjecture that a juxtaposition of ways of thinking had driven G's solution. These may have included "Draw a diagram," "Guess and check," and "Look for relevant relationships among the given quantities." It was shocking to learn that G's score on this problem, as well as on three other problems she solved in a similar manner (i.e., without any "algebraic representation") was zero. Her teacher's justification for this score was something to the effect that G did not solve the problems algebraically, with unknowns and equations, as she was expected to do.

---

[2]We chose not to use the term "heuristics" here because, although every heuristic is a general approach to solving problems, the converse is not true. Heuristics are defined as "rules of thumb for effective problem solving" (Schoenfeld, 1985, p. 23); students' approaches to solving mathematical problems—needless to say—are not always heuristics in this sense.

PROOF SCHEMES

Proving is defined in Harel and Sowder (1998) as the process employed by a person to remove or create doubts about the truth of an observation, and a distinction is made there between ascertaining for oneself and persuading others. A person's *proof scheme* consists of what constitutes ascertaining and persuading for that person. Thus, proof schemes include one's methods of justification. In this sense, "proving" and "justification" are used interchangeably in this article. One of the most ubiquitous proof schemes held by students is the *inductive proof scheme*, where students ascertain for themselves and persuade others about the truth of a conjecture by direct measurements of quantities, numerical computations, substitutions of specific numbers in algebraic expressions, etc. (Harel & Sowder, 1998). We found that this way of thinking governed the way of understanding expressed in Solution 2.1 (Harel, 2001). The way of understanding expressed in Solution 2.2, on the other hand, was found to be a manifestation of a different way of thinking, called *transformational proof scheme*. In Harel (2001) it is shown why Solution 2.1 contains the three essential elements that characterize the transformational proof scheme: (a) consideration of the generality aspects of the conjecture, (b) application of mental operations that are goal oriented and anticipatory—an attempt to predict outcomes on the basis of general principles—and (c) transformations of images that govern the deduction in the evidencing process.[3]

WHAT ARE THE CHARACTERISTICS OF ADVANCED MATHEMATICAL-THINKING?

It is clear that some ways of thinking are flawed (e.g., relying solely on empirical observations to justify mathematical arguments, as we have seen in Solution 2.1; over-generalizing mathematical ideas, as in the common inference students make: "since $2(a + b) = 2a + 2b$ is valid, then $(a + b)^2 = a^2 + b^2$ must also be valid" [Matz, 1980]), although others are sound (e.g., looking for elegant solutions to problems; generalizing mathematical ideas). But in what sense is "mathematical thinking" advanced? Does "advanced" imply "effective," "efficient," or "elegant"? Is nonadvanced mathematical thinking necessarily lacking or faulty? "Advanced" implies there is also an "elementary." If so, in what sense is "mathematical thinking" elementary? It is extremely difficult to characterize these properties, even if we share an intuitive understanding of their meaning, and it is even more difficult to build a taxonomy that differentiates among properties of mathematical thinking. Yet it is of paramount importance to characterize qualities of mathematical thinking to

---

[3]For the full taxonomy of proof schemes, see Harel and Sowder (1998) and Harel (in press).

translate them into essential cognitive objectives—objectives that would position elementary mathematics content for the successful subsequent learning of advanced mathematical content. But what is the complete set of such ways of thinking? Is the set a mere list, or does it have an underlying structure and is it guided by a small number of principles? Advanced mathematical-thinking research can and should take the lead in answering these critical questions. (Heid, Harel, Ferrini-Mundy, & Graham, 2000, p. 35)

One goal of this article is to contribute to our understanding of these issues.

The term "advanced" implies that a developmental process is involved. "Advanced" is, therefore, not an absolute but a relative term, both in relation to a single way of thinking and in relation to different ways of thinking. The attainment of a certain way of thinking is not all or nothing but gradual, and likewise, one might demonstrate a high level of mastery of one way of thinking and little or none of another.

In addition to this relativistic view of the property "advanced," we consider the kind of obstacles one encounters in developing a way of thinking. We adopt Brousseau's distinction between didactical obstacles and epistemological obstacles. The former are the result of narrow or faulty instruction, whereas the latter are unavoidable due to the nature of the development of human knowledge (Brousseau, 1997). But what are the criteria for determining whether the development of a particular type of mathematical thinking necessarily involves epistemological obstacles? Although this question itself requires serious research—cognitive, historical, and epistemological—there already exist some criteria with which to begin a debate on this question. Duroux (1982, cited in Brousseau, 1997) lists necessary conditions for a piece of knowledge to be considered an epistemological obstacle. The first of Duroux's conditions is that epistemological obstacles have traces in the history of mathematics. The second condition is that an epistemological obstacle is not a missing conception, or a lack of knowledge; rather, it is a piece of knowledge or a conception that produces responses that are valid within a particular context, and it generates invalid responses outside this context. To overcome the epistemological obstacle, one must construct a notably different point of view. The third and last condition is that an epistemological obstacle "withstands both occasional contradictions and the establishment of a better piece of knowledge. Possession of a better piece of knowledge is not sufficient for the preceding one to disappear" (Brousseau, 1997, pp. 99–100).

These considerations—the relativistic view of the property "advanced," and the obstacles involved in the developmental process—led us to the following definition, which suggests a research agenda for determining ways of thinking that are advanced, as well as the level of their development:

Mathematical thinking is advanced, if its development involves at least one of the above three conditions for an obstacle to be epistemological. The level of acquisition of a way of thinking by an individual is determined by the extent to which the individual has overcome these obstacles.

It should be noted that the first condition—that an epistemological obstacle must have traces in the history of mathematics—is particularly problematic. It is difficult, and in many cases it may not be possible, to establish whether an obstacle has manifested itself in the history of mathematics. Many obstacles have likely occurred in the historical development of mathematics but have never been observed by historians.

A ready example of an obstacle that satisfies one of Duroux's conditions is the transition from solely additive reasoning to proportional reasoning, a commonly observed difficulty (see discussion following). Also, the notion of epistemological obstacle applies to the construction of both ways of understanding and ways of thinking. For example, the understanding of negative integers and imaginary numbers meets some, if not all three, criteria. The mathematical community of the time (17th century) had to reconstruct—even revolutionize—its ways of thinking about the concepts of number and quantity to accept these new constructs (Klein, 1968; see also Kline, 1972, p. 252).

We conclude this section with two episodes to illustrate the above considerations—not the definition per se.

THE RELATIVISTIC VIEW OF THE
PROPERTY "ADVANCED"

This consideration is discussed in the context of Problems 3–5 below, about a student who can do proportional reasoning but is not yet able to reason in terms of functional representation, and hence does not work in a mathematically efficient fashion.

In a secondary mathematics lesson on exponential decay, the homework included the problem:

Problem 3: The annual rate of inflation in a certain year is 8%. How much will the dollar lose of its purchasing power during this year?

Student H's solution was the following

Solution 3:
H: What costs $1 at the beginning of the year will cost $1.08 at the end of the year. If a product costs $1 at the beginning of the year, that product would cost $1.08 at the end of the year. We want to know how much of the product we can buy for $1 at the end of the year. We are not going to be able to buy the whole product for one dollar, only a portion of it. Let's say we can buy x of it for $1. Then [reasoning proportionally] $1/1.08 = x/1$. $x = 1/1.08 = 1/(1$

$+ 8/100) = 100/108$. We can buy only $100/108 = 92.6\%$ of the product. The dollar lost about 7.4% of its purchasing power.

Following H's presentation of her solution, the teacher introduced the following generalization (without labeling it so):

Problem 4: The annual rate of inflation in a certain year is $a\%$. How much will the dollar lose of its purchasing power during this year?

The teacher went on to present the following solution:

Solution 4:
    Teacher: As H said, a product that costs $1 at the beginning of the year would cost $\$(1 = a/100)$ at the end of the year. Our goal is to find out how much of the product we can buy for $1 at the end of the year. If x is the fraction of the product we can buy for $1, then, as H did, x can be obtained from the equation: $1/(1 + a/100) = x/1$. Solving for x, we get: $x = 1/(1 + a/100) = 100/(100 + a)$, or $100(100/(100 + a))\%$. Thus, if the annual inflation rate is $a\%$, then the dollar loses $(100 - 10000/(100 + a))\%$ of its purchasing power.

Following this work, the teacher discussed with the students the graph of the function $f(a) = 100 - 10000/(100 + a)$, and its physical (economic) meaning. Specifically, he discussed these questions: What are the roots of the function? Where is it defined? What is the behavior of the graph of the function, and what is the economic meaning of these behaviors (e.g., the economic meaning of $a = -100$, or an annual rate of 100% deflation)?
    The next set of homework included the following problem.

Problem 5: During one year, the dollar lost 12.7% of its value. What was the annual rate of inflation during that year?

H applied a similar reasoning to that which she used to solve Problem 3:

Solution 5: At the end of the year, with $1 I can buy only $(100 - 12.7)\% = 87.3/100$ of the product. The whole product would cost $\$y$. $y/1 = 1/(87.3/100)$. $y = 100/87.3 \approx 1.145$. The annual rate of inflation is about 14.5%.

H's solution involves an application of proportional reasoning—a sophisticated way of thinking that warrants the label "advanced," by our definition. First, additive reasoning—an antecedent to proportional reasoning—produces responses that are valid within a particular context but generates invalid responses outside this context. Indeed, the transition from additive reasoning to proportional reasoning requires one to construct a different way of understanding relationships between quantities. Second, research has shown that additive reasoning withstands "occasional contradictions," in that students continue to reason additively after they are shown its inapplicability in certain situations. Finally, the "establishment of a better piece of knowledge," that of proportional reasoning, does not completely remove its application in multiplicative situations—students continue to use it after they have been exposed to the concept of proportionality.

Going back to Solution 5, note that H did not realize that she could obtain the solution by substituting 12.7 for $f(a)$ and solve the equation, $12.7 = 100-10000/(100 + a)$ to obtain the annual rate of inflation a. When she was shown this approach, she had difficulty comprehending it. The latter approach exemplifies a way of mathematical thinking that manifests, among other things, economy of thought. "Economy of thought," in this case, has to do with one's ability to reify Solution 4 into a "solution method." It has been shown that reification is one of the most complex processes in the conceptual development of mathematics—with the individual (e.g., Dubinsky, 1991; Greeno, 1983; Harel & Kaput, 1991) and in the history of mathematics (Sfard, 1992).

It is critical to emphasize that one cannot and would not appreciate the efficiency of the latter solution if he or she has not gone, in various problematic situations, through an elaborated solution, such as that offered by H. Hence, although we desire to label the functional solution as more advanced than the elaborated solution, it may be unlikely that the former could be constructed without the latter. Of course, the student's background plays a critical role. For example, if a student understood functions before studying inflation, the function solution would likely be easier for her. This raises a question that is important to curriculum development and instruction: What possible instructional treatments can help H construct this and other ways of advanced mathematical-thinking?

"Proportional reasoning" and "reification of a solution into a solution method"—the two ways of mathematical thinking that emerged in the analysis of this last problem—are examples of what we, as mathematics educators, feel should be labeled "advanced." This is so because we recognize that these develop during a long period of intellectual effort and have proved essential and effective in doing and creating mathematics. Proportional reasoning, for example, is indispensable in many areas of mathematics, and it demands a reconceptualization of mathematical reality—from a world that is organized solely according to additive principles to a world that is organized according to a differentiation of additive phenomena from multiplicative ones. Noelting (1980a, 1980b) found that even among students who had had the usual instruction dealing with proportions, it was quite common for the students to instead use a unit-rate thinking in working proportion problems, a practice also observed among practicing teachers in the intermediate grades (Harel & Behr, 1995). Lamon (1999) has identified several steps in a possible development of proportional thinking, and Cai and Sun (2002) have described the carefully planned development of proportion in a Chinese curriculum. Arriving at a level of thinking that might be called genuine proportional thinking is not just a matter of telling students about cross-multiplication.

OBSTACLES INVOLVED IN THE
DEVELOPMENTAL PROCESS

This consideration is discussed in the context of Problem 6 below. It shows a major obstacle—to our knowledge little discussed in the literature—that students encounter in building the way of thinking of representing word problems algebraically. The obstacle is not in forming a propositional representation of the problem; rather, its roots seem to lie in the subtle distinction between "variable" and "unknown"—a difficulty that might be appreciated through historical considerations.

Problem 6. Find a point on the number line whose distance from 1 is half its distance from –4.

Solution 6. L, a prospective elementary school teacher, drew a number line and marked on it the points, 1 and –4. After a long pause, L indicated that he did not know what to do next. His teacher proceeded by asking him to describe the problem. In the process of doing so, L indicated—erroneously— that the unknown point couldn't be to the left of 1. It was clear from his description that he understood the problem. L's argument about the location of the unknown point—despite being erroneous—supports this claim.

Teacher: Very good. What is the distance between x and –4?
    L: x plus 4
Teacher: Write that down, please.

L writes $x + 4$.

Teacher: And what is the distance between x and 1?
    L: Half of $x + 4$

L writes $(x + 4)/2$.

Teacher: How else can you express the distance between x and 1?

L reads the problem again.

L: It says it is half the distance from –4.

At this point L was unable to express the distance between x and 1 in a different way from $(x + 4)/2$.

In our experience, the difficulty of forming equations, as in this case, is common among students. A possible conceptual basis for this difficulty is the following. For an expert, a value x representing an unknown in a word problem would involve two ways of understanding. One is expressed in the condition of the problem; the other in the variability of the quantities involved. In our case the condition is "The distance of the unknown point x from 1 is half its distance from –4," and the variability is that of the functional expressions $x + 4$ and $x - 1$. These two ways of understanding are independent of each other. In the former x is an unknown whereas in the latter it is a variable. There might be different explanations for L's difficulty. L may not have constructed these two ways of understanding, may have had difficulty coordinating them, or once he constructed one way of understanding had difficulty attending to the other.

The distinction between "variable" and "unknown" is likely to be more epistemological than didactical—a claim that can be supported by the historical development of the notion of "variable" in the 17th century. As we have discussed earlier, for an obstacle to be epistemological it is necessary that it has occurred in the historical development of mathematics.

WHAT ARE REASONING PRACTICES BY WHICH ADVANCED MATHEMATICAL-THINKING CAN BE ENHANCED?

Our answer to this question is an instructional treatment guided by a system of learning-teaching principles, called the DNR system. The three chief principles of the system are Duality, Necessity, and Repeated Reasoning. In this section we briefly describe the first and last; the middle will be mentioned in the next section. (For the complete description of the system, see Harel, 1998, 2001.)

The Duality Principle.
This principle asserts that
Students' ways of thinking impact their ways of understanding mathematical concepts. Conversely, how students come to understand mathematical content influences their ways of thinking. (Harel, 1998, in press)

Clearly, one's ways of thinking, both good and bad, influence one's further ways of understanding. A student whose way of thinking involves believing that a mathematics story problem should be solved quickly by looking for a key word and then waiting for a teacher's reaction to the answer will certainly derive a different way of understanding for story problems (i.e., will solve them differently) than a student willing to spend several minutes making a drawing, looking for relationships, and then striving for some sort of self-verification. The Duality Principle asserts that the converse is also true, and so teachers and curriculum developers in all grade levels should structure their instruction in a way that provides students with opportunities to construct advanced mathematical-thinking from ways of understanding.

There are powerful examples of the relationship of advanced mathematical-thinking in school mathematics to advanced-mathematical thinking. Consider again the "multiple ways of understanding" we mentioned earlier.

Most students' repertoires of reasoning do not include the way of thinking that "A concept can be understood in different ways," and that "It is often advantageous to change ways of understanding of a concept when attempting to solve a problem." The learning of linear algebra, an advanced-mathematical thinking topic, requires multiple ways of understanding, for one must realize, for example, that problems about systems of linear equations are equivalent to problems about matrices, which, in turn, are equivalent to problems about linear transformations. Students who are not equipped with these ways of thinking are doomed to encounter difficulties. At the precollege level, there are various opportunities to help students think in these ways. The list of ways of understanding fractions mentioned earlier provides one such opportunity. Students should learn, for example, that the fraction 3/4 can be understood in different ways: 3 individual objects, each of quantity 1/4; the result when 3 objects of the same size are shared among 4 individuals; the portion of the quantity 4 that equals the quantity 3; and 3/4 as a mathematical object, a conceptual entity, a number. Similarly, students should become comfortable with the different ways in which many functions can be represented—table, graph, equation, for example—and translations among these representations. Students should also learn that depending on the nature of the problem, some interpretations or representations are more advantageous than others. We believe that it is from these kinds of ways of understanding that students construct the aforementioned ways of thinking.

THE REPEATED REASONING PRINCIPLE

Research has shown that repeated experience, or practice, is a critical factor in enhancing, organizing, and abstracting knowledge (Cooper, 1991). The question is not whether students need to remember facts and master procedures but how they should come to know facts and procedures and how they should practice them. This is the basis for the Repeated Reasoning Principle: "Students must practice reasoning internalize and interiorize specific ways of thinking and ways of under-standing" (Harel, 2001).

Consider again two important ways of thinking we mentioned earlier: "mathematical efficiency" and "transformational proof scheme."

Two elementary school children, S and T, were taught division of fractions. S was taught in a typical method, where he was presented with the rule $(a/b) \div (c/d) = (a/b) \cdot (d/c)$. The rule was introduced to him in a meaningful context and with a mathematically correct justification that he understood, but was asked to repeat. T, on the other hand, was presented with no rule but consistent with the duality principle and the repeated reasoning principle, she was always encouraged to justify her mathematical actions. Each time she encountered a division of fractions problem, she explained its meaning using her understanding of division of whole numbers as the rationale for her solution. S and T were assigned homework problems to compute divisions of fractions. S solved all the problems correctly, and gained, as a result, a good mastery of the division rule. It took T a much longer time to do her homework. Here is what T—a real third-grader—said when she worked on $(4/5) \div (2/3)$:

How many 2/3s in 4/5? I need to find what goes into both [meaning: a unit-fraction that divides 4/5 and 2/3 with no remainders]. 1/15 goes into both. It goes 3 times into 1/5 and 5 times into 1/3, so it would go 12 times into 4/5 and 10 times into 2/3. [She writes: $4/5 = 12/15$; $2/3 = 10/15$; $(4/5) \div (2/3) = (12/15) \div (10/15)$]. How many times does 10/15 go into 12/15? How many times do 10 things go into 12 things? One time and 2/10 of a time, which is 1 and 1/5.

T had opportunities for reasoning of which S was deprived. T practiced reasoning and computation, S practiced only computation. Further, T eventually discovered the division rule and learned an important lesson about mathematical efficiency— a way of thinking S had little chance to acquire.

In Harel and Sowder (1998) we argued that a key to the concept of mathematical proof is the transformational proof scheme—a scheme characterized by consideration of the aspects of the conjecture, application of mental operations that are goal oriented and anticipatory, and transformations of images as part of a deduction process. The education of students toward transformational reasoning must not start in college. Otherwise, years of instruction that focus on the results in mathematics, rather than the reasons behind those results, can leave the impression that only the results are important in mathematics, an opinion sometimes voiced even by university mathematics majors. We argued that instructional activities that educate students to reason transformationally about situations are crucial to students' mathematical development, and that these activities must begin at an early age.

The building of environments in which students regard the giving of reasons as a natural part of mathematics is one of the more exciting aspects of some studies with children in the primary grades (Carpenter, Franke, Jacobs, Fennema, & Empson, 1998; Fuson et al., 2000; Maher & Martino, 1996; Yackel, Cobb, Wood, Wheatley, & Merkel, 1990). Having discussions about which of 2.12 and 2.113 is larger can reveal something important about the children's ways of understanding, and hence, have implications for their ways of thinking. Some may rely erroneously on the number of digits, a way of understanding that naturally develops with whole number work. Or, in comparing 4.21 and 4.238, it may come out that some students focus on the right-most place value and decide that 4.21 is larger because hundredths are larger than thousandths (Resnick et al., 1989). Such discussions would seem to be more valuable in the long run than practicing a teacher-given rule about annexing zeros until each number has the same number of decimal places, especially if the discussions led naturally to the rule.

Similarly, ready-made theorems, formulas, and algorithms, even when motivated and completely proved, are often hastily introduced in undergraduate mathematics courses. An interesting phenomenon was observed in our teaching experiments (Harel, 2001; Harel & Sowder, 1998). It illustrates the importance of practicing mathematical reasoning. Until a mathematical relationship was declared a theorem, the students continued—either voluntarily when they needed to use the relationship or upon request—to justify it. Once the relationship was stated as a theorem, there seemed to be a reduced effort, willingness, and even the ability of some of the students to justify it. This phenomenon was explained in terms of the students' authoritarian view of mathematics (another example of an undesirable, yet common, way of thinking): For them, the label "theorem" renders the relationship into something to obey rather than to reason about. Or, possibly, in the teaching experiment context these students had not practiced enough the reasoning behind the theorem.

WHAT ARE REASONING PRACTICES BY WHICH ADVANCED MATHEMATICAL-THINKING CAN BE HINDERED?

Epistemological obstacles are perhaps more fascinating as objects of scholarly study than didactical obstacles, but we must attend to the latter, for if narrow or faulty instruction leads to problems in thinking or understanding, it should be easier to correct such instruction than it may be to overcome an epistemological obstacle.

Certain teaching practices are still in existence, and even widely used, despite the consensus among mathematics education researchers that they lead to didactical obstacles that are difficult to eradicate. The emphasis on "key" words in instructing students on how to decide what operation to do in solving story problems is an example. Students learn that the phrase "all together" in a problem statement should signal addition; "left" should signal subtraction; "per" should summon multiplication or division, etc. Such instruction, although well intentioned, will give at best short-lived success, and will fail completely if problems are not always written to follow such guides (as in "Thirty rows, with 42 seats in each row, will seat how many, all together?"). More important, these ways of understanding would reinforce faulty ways of thinking—that in doing mathematics what counts is the result, not the reasoning process.

It is fair to say that most instructional planning is a mix of art and science, with art playing the major role. In an effort to be provocative, we challenge some of the usual principles—in our view they are myths—that might guide one's instruction. Like the "key words" approach above, these principles may be helpful in the short run, but may prove to be unhelpful or even counterproductive in the long run. Each of them certainly merits research attention.

Myth 1: In sequencing instruction, start with what is easy.   For example, it is common to introduce methods of solving equations with examples like $x + 2 = 7$ and $3x = 15$. Because these can be solved virtually by inspection, the students may see no need for the usual canons for solving equations, and thus the Necessity Principle (Harel, 1998)—students are more likely to learn when they see a genuine need (intellectual, not necessarily social or economic)—is violated. Much better first examples might be $x + 75.6 = 211.3$ and $1.7x = 27.2$ or even $2.4x + 9.6 = 17.28$, examples not likely to be easily solved by inspection or guessing. In the same vein, perhaps a treatment of congruent figures should start with complicated figures rather than the usual congruence of segments, angles, and triangles. Dienes and Golding long ago suggested that such a "deep-end" approach might be appropriate in many cases:

> At first it is not always wise or useful to present a new mathematical concept in its simplest form .... It has been found that, at least in some cases, it is far better to introduce the new structure at a more difficult level, relying upon the child to discover the less complex sections within the whole structure. (1971, p. 57)

Hence, a building-blocks metaphor in designing curriculum may not be the most useful one, especially if the learner has no idea of the building that will eventually be finished. A more apt metaphor for designing curriculum might be based on some sort of deep-end metaphor, perhaps starting with a picture of the building and the question, "How would you build this?"

Myth 2. The best mental model is a simple one, preferably one quite familiar to the students.   For example, instruction in linear algebra often uses coordinate 2-D and 3-D geometry as the first examples of a vector space. Harel

(1999) argued that these examples constrain students' understanding, so that they think vector space ideas are just ideas about geometry: Linear algebra "=" geometry. Consequently they have difficulty dealing with nongeometric vector spaces. He suggests that using systems of linear equations as a first way of understanding vectors at least keeps the students' thinking in an algebraic domain.

Here is another instance in which starting with the simplest situations may create a didactical obstacle. Multiplication is always introduced as repeated addition; this natural but confining approach seems to lead almost inexorably to the erroneous "multiplication makes bigger" idea (e.g., Fischbein, Deri, Nello, & Marino, 1985; Greer, 1987). Perhaps introducing multiplication as meaning "copies of" would serve the students better (Thompson & Saldanha, 2003): 2×4 tells you how many are in 2 copies of 4, and $2/3 \times 6$ tells you how many are in 2/3 of a copy of 6— thus enveloping repeated-addition and fractional-part-of-an-amount interpretations into one way of thinking about multiplication. We do recognize that other ways of understanding multiplication should also, and usually do, come up in the mathematics curriculum. Such an instructional approach is needed to advance the ways of thinking "a concept can have multiple interpretations" and "it is advantageous to have multiple ways of understanding."

In general, instruction that uses examples limited in some irrelevant or confining way runs the risk of over-generalization, with the irrelevant characteristic perhaps becoming a part of the concept—everyone knows what to draw when asked to draw an "upside-down" trapezoid (cf. Sowder, 1980). The first choices of examples may be crucial, as Marshall's work (1995) with schemas for story problems suggests.

Myth 3. In advanced undergraduate mathematics, begin with the axioms.   Starting with the basic rules of the game might seem sensible, but we feel that the typical undergraduate student is not yet ready to play the game that way. Our argument builds on our notion of "proof scheme" mentioned earlier—a proof scheme guides what one does to convince oneself and to convince others (Harel & Sowder, 1998). Our studies of the proof schemes of undergraduate mathematics majors suggest that extensive earlier work entailing deductions by the student, putting two or more results together to get a new result (deductive proof schemes) must precede any meaningful work with axiomatic developments (axiomatic proof schemes). Otherwise the student may just go through the motions, often rotely, without any genuine appreciation of the development from axioms.

Myth 4. In school practice, use mathematical proofs to convince the students that a mathematical result is certain.   We know that an argument of "but how can you be sure, without a proof" is often used, and that of course mathematicians do look for arguments to assure themselves (and their referees) that the result is indeed established. But mathematicians often look for more than certainty in their proofs—What is the key to the result? Or, does a slight modification in the proof suggest another result? Rav (1999) even claimed that mathematical knowledge is embedded in the proofs, with the theorem only a "headline" (p. 20). But, to repeat an earlier point, we have noticed that a proof for many students is either something to ignore in favor of studying the result, or something only to be dutifully memorized for purposes of repetition on an examination. Indeed, labeling a result with "theorem"—and that labeling alone—often means that the result is certain and requires nothing more, as we noted earlier.

We hypothesize that it is better to emphasize the reasoning, perhaps in several examples, that a proof generalizes. The earlier example in which the child continually utilized a meaning-based argument for calculating divisions by fractions illustrates our point. Brownell (1956) emphasized that the quality of practice, rather than just practice itself, was most important. Carefully planned practice could guide the student's thinking to a higher level. For example, the exercises in Figure 2 could precede, indeed could generate, the result about the relation between the measures of vertical angles, at the same time they are providing practice with the angle sum for a linear pair.

Here is another example of practice paving the way to a result. Suppose the target is one version of the fundamental theorem of calculus: Under certain conditions on f, with F an antiderivative of F, $\int_a^b f(x)dx = F(b) - F(a)$. A common starting point for this version is another version of the fundamental theorem: $\frac{d}{dx} \int_a^x f(t)dt = f(x)$, again with conditions on f. Paraphrasing the latter gives that the integral is an antiderivative of $f(x)$. Hence, for example, $\int_2^x (\cos t)dt$ is the antiderivative of $\cos x$, or cin $x + C$. (Then the practice begins.) Therefore, $\int_2^3 (\cos t)dt = \sin 3 + C$, but $\int_2^2 (\cos t)dt = \sin 2 + C = 0$, so $C = -\sin 2$, and $\int_2^3 (\cos t)dt = \sin 3 + C = \sin 3 - \sin 2$. Repetitions of the argument with other integrals sets the stage for the general argument (= proof) that $\int_a^b f(x)dx = F(b) - F(a)$, with $F(x)$ an antiderivative of $f(x)$.

Find the measurements x and y.

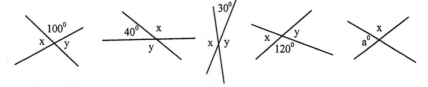

FIGURE 2   Practice leading to a general result.

Opportunity to Learn

The most serious didactical obstacle is a lack of opportunity to learn. In particular, we have in mind the (good) ways of thinking and understanding mentioned earlier, and the "habits of mind" of Cuoco, Goldenberg, and Marks (1996). Instruction (or a curriculum) that ignores sense-making, for example, can scarcely be expected to produce sense-making students. Computational shortcuts like "move the decimal point" or "cross-multiply" or "invert and multiply" given as rules without any attention as to why these work turns elementary school mathematics into what is deservedly called a bag of tricks. Also, students who never have a chance to make conjectures cannot become more skilled at conjecturing—and it may be hypothesized that students who have never conjectured do not see any need for mathematical proof. And so on.

Not an Exclusive Or

Whether a particular obstacle to learning is didactical or epistemological, in an exclusive-or sense, is, we believe, too limiting. Harel (in press) offers the view that an obstacle may be partly didactical and partly epistemological. Consider, for example, "multiplication makes bigger" (MMB), the well-documented misconception mentioned earlier that is an obstacle for many students (through college) in choosing an operation for solving a story problem (Greer, 1987). MMB clearly meets Duroux's partially-valid and obstinacy criteria, and one might argue that it also has historical roots, with multiplication probably first formalized with whole numbers. Yet, MMB could perhaps have its influence allayed, if not nullified, by some instructional modification like some more-inclusive view, say the "copies of" interpretation mentioned earlier, or perhaps by exploring "what it would be" via a calculator calculation of something like 0.2×15 or $(1/2)x24$ at an age before extensive experience with whole numbers leads to MMB. Hence, MMB might be positioned on a didactical versus epistemological set of axes as in Figure 3.

In a similar way, one can conjecture difficulties with proportional reasoning, with understanding $(-1)(-1) = +1$, with linear independence, or with some notational conventions like $\sin^{-1} x$, as being both didactical and epistemological in nature, as we have speculated in Figure 4.

SUMMARY

Our view is that the roots of mathematical thinking for advanced mathematics must be fostered during the study of elementary mathematics. General ways of thinking, built on rich ways of understanding in elementary mathematics, can then symbiotically support further ways of understanding and of thinking in advanced

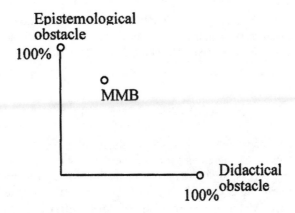

FIGURE 3   Multiplication makes bigger (MMB) as a mix of obstacles.

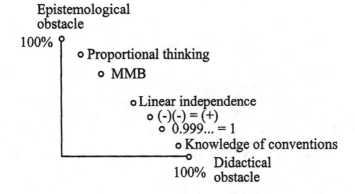

FIGURE 4   Hypothesized mixes of types of obstacles.

mathematics. Obstacles to ways of thinking and ways of understanding may be epistemological and/or didactical, with didactical obstacles more easily identified and perhaps more easily overcome than epistemological obstacles. We propose that a way of mathematical thinking be called "advanced" if its development necessarily involves at least one of the three necessary conditions for epistemological obstacles identified by Duroux (1982, cited in Brousseau, 1997). An important next step will be to identify ways of thinking that meet this criterion.

We endorse the DNR-based instruction for furthering ways of thinking and ways of understanding: (Duality Principle) make the dually supportive roles of ways of thinking and ways of understanding a conscious, carefully planned part of the cognitive objectives for coursework in mathematics; (Necessity Principle) build instruction via problems that contain intellectual appeal to the students; and (Repeated Reasoning Principle) involve repeated reasoning to give a firm foundation for ways of thinking and ways of understanding. Finally, by labeling them "myths," we offer a critique of some teaching "axioms" that have face validity but might actually hinder the development of fruitful ways of thinking and ways of understanding.

ACKNOWLEDGMENTS

Some of the ideas presented in this article are the result of National Science Foundation Project 9355861; opinions expressed here, of course, are those of the authors and are not necessarily those of the Foundation. We also acknowledge with gratitude the clarifying conversations with Alfred Manaster, and the suggestions from the Advanced Mathematical Thinking Group of PME–NA, particularly those at the Tucson meeting: Stacy Brown, Walter Houston, Kathy Ivey, Barbara Loud, Denise Mewborn, and Sharon Walen.

REFERENCES

Brousseau, G. (1997). *Theory of didactical situations in mathematics* (N. Balacheff, M. Cooper, R. Sutherland, & V. Warfield, Eds. & Trans.). Dordrecht, The Netherlands: Kluwer Academic.

Brownell, W. A. (1956). Meaning and skill—Maintaining the balance. *Arithmetic Teacher, 3*, 129–136.

Cai, J., & Sun, W. (2002). Developing students' proportional reasoning: A Chinese perspective. In B. Litwiller & G. Bright (Eds.), *Making sense of fractions, ratios, and proportions* (pp. 195–205). Reston, VA: National Council of Teachers of Mathematics.

Carpenter, T. C., Franke, M. L., Jacobs, V. R., Fennema, E., & Empson, S. (1998). A longitudinal study of invention and understanding in children's multidigit addition and subtraction. *Journal for Research in Mathematics Education, 29*, 3–20.

Cooper, R. (1991). The role of mathematics transformation and practice in mathematical development. In L. P. Steffe (Ed.), *Epistemological foundations in mathematical experience* (pp. 102–123). New York: Springer-Verlag.

Cuoco, A., Goldenberg, E. P, & Marks, J. (1996). Habits of mind: An ongoing principle for mathematics curricula. *Journal of Mathematical Behavior, 15*, 375–402.

Dienes, Z. P., & Golding, G. W. (1971). *Approach to modern mathematics*. New York: Herder and Herder.

Dubinsky, E. (1991). Reflective abstraction in advanced mathematical thinking. In D. Tall (Ed.), *Advanced mathematical thinking* (pp. 95–102). Dordrecht, The Netherlands: Kluwer Academic.

Fischbein, E., Deri, M., Nello, M. S., & Marino, M. S. (1985). The role of implicit models in solving verbal problems in multiplication and division. *Journal for Research in Mathematics Education, 16*, 3–17.

Fuson, K. C., De La Cruz, Y., Smith, S. T., Cicero, A. M. L., Hudson, K., Pilar, R., et al. (2000). Blending the best of the twentieth century to achieve a mathematics equity pedagogy in the twenty-first century. In M. J. Burke & F. R. Curcio (Eds.), *Learning mathematics for a new century* (pp. 197–212). Reston, VA: National Council of Teachers of Mathematics.

Greeno, J. (1983). Conceptual entities. In D. Genter & A. L. Stevens (Eds.), *Mental models* (pp. 227–252). Hillsdale, NJ: Lawrence Erlbaum Associates, Inc.

Greer, B. (1987). Nonconservation of multiplication and division involving decimals. *Journal for Research in Mathematics Education, 18*, 37–45.

Harel, G. (1998). Two dual assertions: The first on learning and the second on teaching (or vice versa). *The American Mathematical Monthly, 105*, 497–507.

Harel, G. (1999). Students' understanding of proofs: A historical analysis and implications for the teaching of geometry and linear algebra. *Linear Algebra and Its Applications, 302–303*, 601–613.

Harel, G. (2001). The development of mathematical induction as a proof scheme: A model for *DNR*-based instruction. In S. Campbell & R. Zazkis (Eds.), *Learning and teaching number theory* (pp. 185–212). Westport, CT: Ablex.

Harel, G. (in press). Students' proof schemes revisited: Historical and epistemological considerations. In P. Boero (Ed.), *Theorems in school*. Dordrecht, The Netherlands: Kluwer Academic.

Harel, G., & Behr, M. (1995). Teachers' solutions for multiplicative problems. *Hiroshima Journal for Research in Mathematics Education, 3*, 31–51.

Harel, G., & Kaput, J. (1991). The role of conceptual entities and their symbols in building advanced mathematical concepts. In D. Tall (Ed.), *Advanced mathematical thinking* (pp. 65–79). Dordrecht, The Netherlands: Kluwer Academic.

Harel, G., & Sowder, L. (1998). Student's proof schemes: Results from exploratory studies. In A. H. Schoenfeld, J. Kaput, & E. Dubinsky (Eds.), *Research in collegiate mathematics education. III* (pp. 234–283). Providence, RI: American Mathematical Society.

Heid, M. K., Harel, G., Ferrini-Mundy, J., & Graham, K. (2000). Advanced mathematical thinking: Implications of various perspectives on advanced mathematical thinking for mathematics education reform. In M. L. Fernandez (Ed.), *Proceedings of the 22nd Annual Meeting of the North American Chapter of the International Group for the Psychology of Mathematics Education* (Vol. 1, pp. 33–37). Columbus, OH: ERIC Clearinghouse for Science, Mathematics, and Environmental Education.

Klein, J. (1968). *Greek mathematical thought and the origin of algebra*. New York: Dover.

Kline, M. (1972). *Mathematical thought from ancient to modern times*. New York: Oxford University Press.

Lamon, S. J. (1999). Ratio and proportion: Elementary didactical phenomenology. In J. Sowder & B. Schappelle (Eds.), *Providing a foundation for teaching mathematics in the middle grades* (pp. 167–198). Albany: State University of New York Press.

Maher, C. A., & Martino, A. M. (1996). The development of the idea of mathematical proof: A 5-year case study. *Journal for Research in Mathematics Education, 27*, 194–214.

Marshall, S. P. (1995). *Schemas in problem solving*. New York: Cambridge University Press.

Matz, M. (1980). Toward a computational theory of algebraic competence. *Journal of Mathematical Behavior, 3*, 93–166.

Noelting, G. (1980a). The development of proportional reasoning and the ratio concept, Part I—Differentiation of stages. *Educational Studies in Mathematics, 11*, 217–253.

Noelting, G. (1980b). The development of proportional reasoning and the ratio concept, Part II—Problem-Structure at successive stages; problem-solving strategies and the mechanism of adaptive restructuring. *Educational Studies in Mathematics, 11*, 331–363.

Rav, Y. (1999). Why do we prove theorems? *Philosophia Mathematica, 7*, 5–41.

Resnick, L. B., Nesher, P., Leonard, F., Magone, M., Omanson, S., & Peled, I. (1989). Conceptual bases of arithmetic errors: The case of decimal fractions. *Journal for Research in Mathematics Education, 20*, 8–27.

Schoenfeld, A. H. (1985). *Mathematical problem solving*. Orlando, FL: Academic Press.

Sfard, A. (1992). Operational origins of mathematical objects and the quandary of reification—The case of function. In E. Dubinsky & G. Harel (Eds.), *The concept of function: Aspects of epistemology and pedagogy* (pp. 59–84). MAA Notes No. 25. Washington, DC: Mathematical Association of America.

Sowder, L. (1980). Concept and principle learning. In R. J. Shumway (Ed.), *Research in mathematics education* (pp. 244–285). Reston, VA: National Council of Teachers of Mathematics.

Thompson, P. W., & Saldanha, L. (2003). Fractions and multiplicative reasoning. In J. Kilpatrick, W. G. Martin, & D. Schifter (Eds.), *A research companion to "Principles and Standards for School Mathematics"* (pp. 95–113). Reston, VA: National Council of Teachers of Mathematics.

Yackel, E., Cobb, P., Wood, T., Wheatley, G., & Merkel, G. (1990). The importance of social interaction in children's construction of mathematical knowledge. In T. J. Cooney & C. R. Hirsch (Eds.), *Teaching and learning mathematics in the 1990s* (pp. 12–21). Reston, VA: National Council of Teachers of Mathematics.

MATHEMATICAL THINKING AND LEARNING, 7(1), 51–73

Advancing Mathematical Activity: A Practice-Oriented View of Advanced Mathematical Thinking

Chris Rasmussen
Department of Mathematics and Statistics
San Diego State University

Michelle Zandieh
Department of Mathematics and Statistics
Arizona State University

Karen King
Department of Mathematics
Michigan State University

Anne Teppo
Department of Mathematical Sciences
Montana State University

The purpose of this article is to contribute to the dialogue about the notion of *advanced mathematical thinking* by offering an alternative characterization for this idea, namely advancing mathematical activity. We use the term *advancing* (versus *advanced*) because we emphasize the progression and evolution of students' reasoning in relation to their previous activity. We also use the term *activity*, rather than *thinking*. This shift in language reflects our characterization of progression in mathematical thinking as acts of participation in a variety of different socially or culturally situated mathematical practices. For these practices, we emphasize the changing nature of students' mathematical activity and frame the process of progression in terms of multiple layers of horizontal and vertical mathematizing.

Mathematics education research dealing with the learning and teaching of undergraduate mathematics is an emerging area of interest. Some have considered the

Requests for reprints should be sent to Chris Rasmussen, Department of Mathematics and Statistics, San Diego State University, San Diego, CA 92182-7720. E-mail:chrisra@sciences.sdsu.edu

area of undergraduate mathematics education to be different from K–12 mathematics education because there are more opportunities for what might be thought of as "advanced mathematical thinking." What constitutes advanced mathematical thinking, however, continues to be debated. Does this phrase mean thinking about advanced topics? Does it mean thinking in "advanced" ways about any mathematics? Might it mean something different?

Tall (1992) described advanced mathematical thinking as composed of two components—the specification of concepts by precise mathematical definitions (including statements of axioms) and the logical deductions of theorems based upon them. In addition, Tall stated, "In taking students through the transition to advanced mathematical thinking, we should realize that the formalizing and systematizing of the mathematics is the final stage of mathematical thinking, not the *total activity*" (pp. 508–509, emphasis added). We agree with Tall on this point, and in our research we seek ways to characterize students' total activity as they progress in their mathematical sophistication.

The purpose of this article is to contribute to the dialogue about the notion of advanced mathematical thinking. In particular, we offer an alternative characterization of advanced mathematical thinking that focuses on important mathematical practices and qualitatively different types of activities within these practices. Our characterization of advanced mathematical thinking, that we refer to as *advancing mathematical activity*, is not limited to specific grade or content levels.

We use the term *advancing* rather than *advanced* because we address the process of students' total activity rather than just the "final stage" referred to by Tall. This shift from characterizing "advanced" as a final state to characterizing advanced as a relative term illuminates aspects of students' progression and evolution of reasoning, in relation to their previous activity. Our emphasis on advanc*ing*, rather than on advanc*ed*, also limits the evaluative nature that often comes with the term advanced. In particular, we refrain from characterizing individuals as "advanced" or "not advanced." In our opinion, such characterizations minimize the potentials for all learners, not just the few in upper-level undergraduate courses, to progress in their mathematical sophistication.

We also use the term *activity*, rather than *thinking*. This shift in language reflects our characterization of progression in mathematical thinking as acts of participation in a variety of different socially or culturally situated mathematical practices (Lave & Wenger, 1991; Sfard, 1998; Wenger, 1998). Students' symbolizing, algorithmatizing, and defining activities are three examples of such social or cultural practices. These three mathematical practices are not meant to be exhaustive, but represent a useful set of core practices that cut across all mathematical domains. Another significant mathematical practice, one that we leave to later analysis, is justifying.

The term *thinking* is often used, from a psychological point of view, to describe mathematical growth. Although this focus on thinking often provides useful insights into inferred cognitive structures, it can result in neglecting the types of mathematical activities and ways of participating in these activities that foster and promote progressively sophisticated mathematical reasoning. Because we view learning as acts of participation in different mathematical practices, we intentionally use the term *activity* rather than *thinking*. Our use of the term activity, however, does not reflect a dichotomy between thinking and doing but rather intends to encompass both. We view the relationship between doing and thinking to be reflexive in nature, not dichotomous. As students engage in particular activities, they not only enact their understandings but also enlarge their thinking and ways of reasoning in the process. This is what we mean when we say that the students' symbolizing, algorithmatizing, and defining activities encompass both doing and thinking.

To summarize, our use of the term *activity* reflects a view that mathematics is first and foremost a human activity (Freudenthal, 1991), in which doing and thinking are dualities situated within particular social or cultural practices. As argued by Cobb and Bowers (1999), the notion of participating in practices

is not restricted to face-to-face interactions with others. Instead, all individual actions are viewed as elements or aspects of an encompassing system of social practices and individuals are viewed as participating in social practices, even when they act in physical isolation from others. (p. 5)

In building on the work of theorists such as Cobb and Bowers (1999) and Lave and Wenger (1991), our efforts in this paper are in line with Tall's (1991) statement, "in trying to formulate helpful ways of looking at advanced mathematical thinking, it is important that we take a broad view and try to see the illumination that various theories can bring" (p. 21). In the sections that follow, we first develop the notion of advancing mathematical activity as acts of participation in different mathematical practices by adapting and modifying Treffers' (1987) constructs of horizontal and vertical mathematizing. We then describe the research projects from which we draw examples. Next, we illustrate and clarify our constructs of horizontal and vertical mathematizing with examples of students' symbolizing, algorithmatizing, and defining activities. In the final section we discuss the links and parallels between the three practices with respect to horizontal and vertical mathematizing, and conclude with some remarks about the utility of these notions for improving mathematics education.

ADVANCING MATHEMATICAL ACTIVITY

Mathematical learning means participating in different types of mathematical practices. To explicate important variations within each practice, we modify Treffers' (1987) idea of progressive mathematizing. Treffers describes progressive mathematizing in terms of a sequence of two types of mathematical activity—horizontal mathematizing and vertical mathematizing. We emphasize that, like doing and thinking, we view horizontal and vertical mathematizing as reflexively related, not as dichotomies. As we make clear in the discussion that follows, the distinction between horizontal and vertical activity is a relative one, one that cannot be made without the other. This reflexivity is a strength because it enables us to make comparisons about the nature of students' activity and it provides us with a language in which to talk about the process by which students develop new views and sensitivities.

According to Treffers (1987), horizontal mathematizing is described as "transforming a problem field into a mathematical problem" (p. 247). This notion of horizontal mathematizing suggests that, for Treffers, what constitutes a problem field is nonmathematical (i.e., some context related to a real-world situation). We treat horizontal mathematizing more broadly to include problem fields or situations that are, from the perspective of those involved, already mathematical in nature. In our view, what constitutes a problem field or problem situation depends on the background, experiences, and goals of those engaged in the mathematical activity. Thus, what constitutes a problem situation for learners in a real analysis course is potentially different from that for learners in an elementary school classroom. Our stance on the relativity of what might be taken as the context for horizontal mathematizing is certainly not a new idea. Dewey (1910/1991) posited that the distinction between what is concrete and what is abstract is relative to the intellectual progress of the person. Indeed, we find the notion of a "final stage" unhelpful in thinking about students' mathematical development because no matter what the intellectual progress, there is always room for growth.

In our broadening of what is meant by a problem field, *horizontal mathematizing* refers to formulating a problem situation in such a way that it is amenable to further mathematical analysis. Thus, horizontal mathematizing might include, but not be limited to, activities such as experimenting, pattern snooping, classifying, conjecturing, and organizing.

Given the situatedness of horizontal mathematizing, vertical mathematizing is then only understood in relation to students' current activity. *Vertical mathematizing* consists of those activities that are grounded in and built on horizontal activities. Thus, vertical mathematizing might include activities such as reasoning about abstract structures, generalizing, and formalizing. Students' new resulting mathematical realities may then be the context for further horizontal mathematizing. To clarify, vertical mathematizing activities serve the purpose of creating new mathematical realities for the students. These new mathematical realities can then be the context or ground for further horizontal and/or vertical mathematizing activities, producing a sequence or chain of progressive mathematizations.

Thus, progressive mathematizing can involve multiple layers of horizontal and vertical mathematizing activities. In the simplest sense, progressive mathematizing refers to a shift or movement from horizontal activities to vertical activities. This shift is not necessarily uni-directional, as vertical activities often "fold back" (Pirie

& Kieren, 1994) to horizontal activities. In more complex cases, progressive mathematizing refers to the fact that students' newly formed mathematical realities, resulting from previous mathematizing, can be the context for additional horizontal and/or vertical mathematizing. This more complex aspect of progressive mathematizing is touched on in the algorithmatizing and defining sections.

Another, and perhaps more significant modification we make to the ideas of horizontal and vertical mathematizing, and one that has been implicit in the preceding discussion and that we now make explicit, is framing progressive mathematizing not in terms of particular ideas such as fractions or long division, as Treffers (1987) does, but in terms of socially and culturally situated mathematical practices. In our view, the mathematical practices of symbolizing, algorithmatizing, and defining are mechanisms by which particular ideas such as fraction, long division, solutions to differential equations, or triangle evolve. This is a nontrivial modification because it calls for attention to the types of activities in which learners engage for the purpose of building new mathematical ideas and methods for solving problems.

In summary, the notion of advancing mathematical activity is the building and progression of practices. Participation in these practices, and changes in these practices, is synonymous with learning (Cobb & Bowers, 1999; Lave & Wenger, 1991). The process by which these practices build and progress is referred to as progressive mathematization, with its multiple layers of horizontal and vertical types of activity. As alluded to earlier, the separation of mathematical activity into horizontal and vertical aspects is somewhat artificial, as in reality the two activities are closely related. However, for the purposes of clarifying the nature of advancing mathematical activity and its progression, this distinction proves useful. As described in the next section, our tightly integrated research, teaching, and instructional design work has provided a unique setting from which the construct of advancing mathematical activity has grown.

RESEARCH SETTING

We have emphasized in our classroom-based research in undergraduate mathematics education the idea of progressive mathematizing and we therefore draw on examples from different classroom teaching experiments (two in differential equations at a mid-sized public university and one in Euclidean and nonEuclidean geometry at a large public university[1]) to illustrate the notion of advancing mathematical activity. The methodological approach we took in these research efforts is that of the class-

---

[1]The researchers who participated in some or all of the differential equations teaching experiments were Karen King, Chris Rasmussen, Michelle Stephan, and Erna Yackel. The researchers that participated in the geometry teaching experiment were Barbara Edwards, Libby Krussel, Chris Rasmussen, and Michelle Zandieh.

room teaching experiment, as described by Cobb (2000). Data consisted of videorecordings of each class session, videorecorded interviews with individual students, copies of students' written work, and records of project meetings. These classroom teaching experiments had two overarching goals. One goal was to develop paradigmatic case studies of the processes by which students develop particular mathematical ideas in relation to the norms and practices established in their classroom communities. A second related goal was an interest in examining the viability of adapting to the university setting instructional and curriculum design approaches that have been effective for promoting student learning of K–12 mathematics.

In all of these teaching experiments we paid particular attention to the social aspects of the classroom, using Cobb and Yackel's (1996) interpretive framework for coordinating sociological and psychological points of view. Various sociological aspects of this research, including classroom norms pertaining to explanation and classroom mathematical practices, are reported elsewhere (see Rasmussen, Yackel, & King, 2003; Stephan & Rasmussen, 2002; Yackel, Rasmussen, & King, 2000). To a large extent in the differential equations teaching experiment and to a smaller extent in the geometry teaching experiment, the research team's instructional design efforts were grounded in the instructional design theory of Realistic Mathematics Education (Freudenthal, 1973; Gravemeijer, 1994, 1999). The interpretive framework for making sense of the complexity of the classroom learning environment and the instructional design theory of Realistic Mathematics Education were critical to the success of these classroom teaching experiments.

We use examples from our teaching experiments to illustrate and clarify our theoretical development of the notion of advancing mathematical activity, bringing to the fore aspects of horizontal and vertical mathematizing activities within the practices of symbolizing, algorithmatizing, and defining. Rather than primarily viewing mathematics as a set and preorganized discipline that is carefully articulated to students, these three mathematical practices constitute a key collection of activities through which learners can create, organize, and systematize mathematics.

SYMBOLIZING

To better understand how symbolizing can be viewed as a mathematical practice with horizontal and vertical mathematizing aspects, it is useful to first consider some general orienting comments on the nature of symbolizing and symbols. The perspective we take toward symbolizing both departs from and connects with the way that Herscovics (1996) described symbolizing (Rasmussen, 1999). Herscovics wrote that symbolizing

provides the means to detach a concept from its concrete embodiments. However, the introduction of symbols can be premature if an adequate intuitive basis is lacking…. Thus mathematical notation can be meaningful only when it is used in the process of *mathematizing* previously acquired informal knowledge. (p. 358, emphasis added)

We connect with Herscovics' suggestion that symbolizing is a key aspect of mathematizing and we elaborate horizontal and vertical aspects of such activity. However, instead of viewing symbolizing as a means to "detach a concept from its concrete embodiments" (Herscovics, 1996, p. 358), that is reminiscent of perspectives that treat one's reasoning about mathematical concepts and their representations as separate, distinct entities, we view students' conceptual development and the activity of symbolizing as reflexively related (Gravemeijer, Cobb, Bowers, & Whitenack, 2000; Meira, 1995). In this approach, "it is while actually engaging in the activity of symbolizing that symbolizations emerge and develop meaning within the social setting of the classroom" (Gravemeijer et al., 2000, p. 235–236). From this point of view, the need for notation and symbolism arises in part as a means to record reasoning and serves as an impetus to further students' mathematical development. In this way, symbolizing is less a process of detachment and more a process of creation and reinvention. Further mathematizing activity and powerful use of conventional symbols emerge from and are grounded in students' previous symbolizing activities.[2]

In the following paragraphs excerpts taken from a classroom teaching experiment in a university-level differential equations course are used to illustrate aspects of advancing mathematical activity within the practice of symbolizing. In these examples, the symbolizing activities in which students' engage shift from recording and communicating their thinking to using their symbolizations as inputs for further mathematical reasoning and conceptualization. This progression in symbolizing is reflective of the horizontal to vertical mathematizing progression and exemplifies our notion of advancing mathematical activity.

Symbolizing: Horizontal Mathematizing

In the first example students were analyzing solution functions to the differential equation $\frac{dP}{dt} = 0.6P\left(1 - \frac{P}{12.3}\right)$ Their primary tool at this point was the slope field, such as the one shown in Figure 1a. Part of the discussion between the teacher and students focused on the possibility of a particular solution function graph, such as that shown in Figure 1b.

---

[2]This perspective on symbolizing is compatible with Nemirovsky's (1994) notion of symbol-use, that refers to the actual use of mathematical symbols by someone, for a purpose, and as part of a chain of meaningful events.

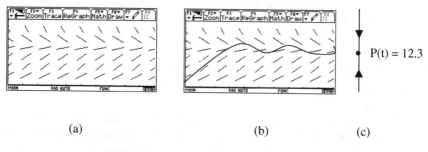

(a)   (b)   (c)

FIGURE 1   Slope field for dP/dt = 0.6P(1 − P/12.3).

Students reasoned that such a solution function was not possible. The following reasoning was typical of the explanations offered by them.

> Joe: I don't think the function would oscillate because if it did then after the function was bigger than 12.3 the slope would still be positive, but from the differential equation and the slope field I know that the slopes are negative when you're above 12.3. So that can't happen.

After further discussion and elaboration, what experts in differential equations understand to be a (partial) phase line was intentionally introduced by the teacher to record students' reasoning, as shown in Figure 1c. From the students' perspective, what the teacher sketched did not yet have a name and was simply a notational device that was consistent with their mathematical reasoning about the behavior of solution functions for the given differential equation. Thus, the symbolizing activity, that was initiated on the part of the teacher in response to student reasoning, is horizontal in nature because this activity seeks to formulate symbolically the given problem situation and students' mathematical reasoning within this situation.

The next example we discuss is a problem given to students on an exam. The task (shown in Figure 2) was a novel one for students, as they had not previously experienced problems of this form. Thus, the work of a student named Kevin[3] that we provide and the symbolizing that this student used are unlikely to be the result of a memorized procedure. This example is different from the previous example in two ways. First, the phase line is now a student record rather than a teacher record, indicating ownership of the inscription. Second, the phase line is used to communicate the long-term behavior of several solution functions, rather that just one solution function. The use of the phase line to communicate the behavior of many solution functions (i.e., the structure of the solution space) is important because it

---

[3]All names are pseudonyms.

Suppose a population of Nomads is modeled by the differential equation $\dfrac{dN}{dt} = f(N)$. The graph of dN/dt is shown below (CAUTION: this is NOT a graph of a solution function, it is a graph of the right-hand side of the autonomous differential equation)

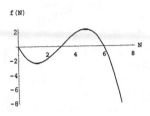

Graph of $f(N)$ vs. N

For the following values of the initial population, what is the long-term value of the population? Be sure to briefly explain your reasoning.

    (i) $N(0) = 2$,   (ii) $N(0) = 3$,   (iii) $N(0) = 4$,   (iv) $N(0) = 7$

FIGURE 2   Student response on novel task.

provides the background for vertical mathematizing in which students use the phase line to infer changes to the structure of the solution space.

    The task was to determine the long-term value of a population for various initial populations given a particular differential equation. The novel aspect of the task was that students were provided only with a graph of the differential equation, rather than the equation itself. This circumvented the direct use of a slope field to symbolize and/or reason about the situation and provided an opportunity for them to symbolize (if they so chose) the situation in ways meaningful to them.

    As shown in Figure 3, Kevin began his response by interpreting the given information. For example, he wrote, "when the population of nomads is less than 3, the rate of change of nomads with respect to time will decrease [sic, is negative] until they become extinct." He made similar statements about other ranges for the initial population and then made specific conclusions about the long-term value of the population for specific initial populations.

    As shown in Figure 3, Kevin used a phase line in his response. We interpret his use of a phase line as a means to formulate, record, support, and communicate his reasoning. As such, we view this as another example of horizontal mathematizing. We infer that, for this student, the phase line signified the evolution of all solution functions. In this way, the phase line began to take on conceptual meaning independent of the population context. The next example is illustrative of how symbols such as the phase line, that in this case originated as a means to record student reasoning, can shift in function with students' progressive mathematizing activities.

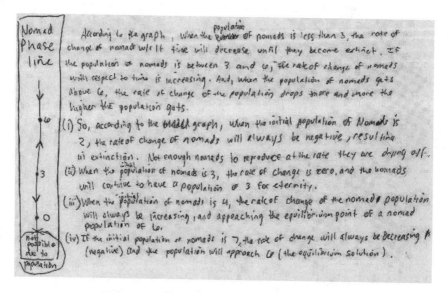

FIGURE 3   Student response.

Symbolizing: Vertical Mathematizing

In the following example we illustrate a vertical mathematizing aspect of symbolizing. In particular, we discuss how this particular student, Joaquin, used results of previous symbolizing activities as input for other symbolizing activities in a dynamic and relational manner. Joaquin's symbolizing activity built on the prior activity with the phase line to generate new mathematical ideas. The vertical nature of this student's work, when contrasted with the previous two symbolizing examples, comes into full view.

The problem, that appears in the textbook by Blanchard, Devaney, and Hall (1998), asks students to identify the bifurcation values of α for the differential equation $\frac{dy}{dt} = y^6 - 2y^4 + \alpha$ and to describe the bifurcations that take place as α increases. At the start of his response, Joaquin noted that whenever the rate of change equation is negative, $y(t)$ will decrease and whenever the rate of change equation is positive, $y(t)$ will increase. This conclusion results in his symbolizing four different regions as shown in Figure 4 where $y(t)$ is either increasing or decreasing.

Our interpretation of his reasoning is that he conceptualized the space of solution functions as being partitioned into four regions separated by three equilibrium solution functions. His references to $y(t)$ and his informal use of notation signifying various solution functions $y(t)$, as shown in Figure 4, support this interpretation.

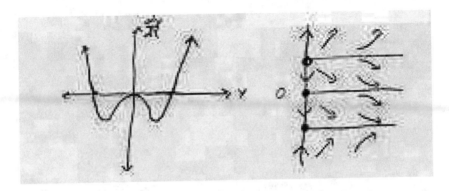

FIGURE 4   Student response on bifurcation task.

At this point, we characterize Joaquin's symbolizing in Figure 4 as horizontal mathematizing because the various representations he used serve to essentially formulate and communicate the problem situation when $\alpha = 0$. Symbolizing is used to create a model-of the situation (Gravemeijer et al. 2000; Rasmussen, 1999). As Joaquin varied α, he used these symbolizations dynamically as input for further symbolizations. We take the latter part of his response as characteristic of vertical mathematizing, that creates a model-for reasoning relationally.

More specifically, Joaquin varied the value of α, that he determined "will shift the graph up or down along the dy/dt axis," as shown in his sketch in Figure 5a. Joaquin then concluded that "Qualitatively, there are five types possible." He then found the specific values of α that result in a bifurcation and made a differentiation between these types. The student symbolized the different types with five different phase lines, as shown in Figure 5b. Joaquin's use of the word "type" is significant for it suggests that for him, each phase line signified all of the solution functions corresponding to each particular value of α. Moreover, each of the five different phase lines is qualitatively different. For example, the first phase line in Figure 5b where $\alpha < 0$ consists of three different regions separated by two equilibrium solutions. The second phase line where $\alpha = 0$ consists of four different regions separated by three equilibrium solutions, and so on. Joaquin then explained how the different phase lines relate to each other and how the equilibria change dynamically as α changes. It is in this sense, as we said earlier, that Joaquin's symbolizing was relational in manner. For example, he stated that "Taking α smaller from graph C (when $0 < \alpha < 1.185$), c_1 and c_2 spread apart as b_1 and b_2 approach each other" (where c_1, c_2, b_1, and b_2 all refer to equilibrium solutions). Joaquin's description of two equilibrium solutions spreading apart as α varies and the other two equilibrum solutions approaching each other strongly suggest that his reasoning was based on a dynamic image of the phase line.

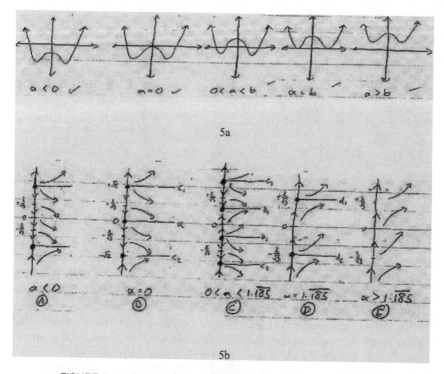

5a

5b

FIGURE 5   Student response on bifurcation task (continued from Figure 4).

Moreover, Joaquin described elsewhere that he had an "epiphany" about how to use the graph of the rate of change equation to figure out the exact bifurcation values. He symbolized, using a sequence of static graphs, a dynamic image of the rate of change equation, as shown in Figure 5a, and he figured out for himself that the key was to determine where the extrema of dy/dt are tangent to the y-axis. Joaquin's use of the word epiphany to describe his reasoning indicates that his solution was not the result of a memorized procedure. It appears that Joaquin had developed a highly integrated and complex way of reasoning about the space of solution functions to differential equations and had developed effective and dynamic symbolizations to foster and further his reasoning.

Taken together, these two examples illustrate how the practice of symbolizing can be viewed as a process of advancing mathematical activity. Indicative of horizontal mathematizing, the phase line was first used as a device to record and communicate student reasoning and conclusions. In the latter part of the second example, this symbol became a tool for reasoning about the generalized space of solution functions in a dynamic manner. Thus, in relation to students' previous activity, this shift represents a form of vertical mathematizing that builds on and extends previous horizontal mathematizing activity. In the following section, a similar progression in activity from horizontal mathematizing to vertical mathematizing is illustrated for the practice of algorithmatizing.

ALGORITHMATIZING

Much of the traditional K–14 mathematics curriculum focuses on students' acquisition of algorithms to do particular types of problems. From double-digit subtraction with regrouping to integration by parts, students' responses across a variety of problems demonstrate that they have acquired these algorithms and can reproduce the appropriate procedures when these procedures are required. As Berlinski (2000) notes, "Algorithms are human artifacts" (p. xvii), the product of human activity. Keeping this activity perspective of algorithms in the forefront suggests that instead of focusing on the acquisition of these algorithms, we can characterize learning to use and understand algorithms as participating in the practice of algorithmatizing. By examining the activity that leads to the creation and use of artifacts, as opposed to the acquisition of the artifacts, we view mathematical learning of and in reference to algorithms through a different lens. This is not to say that the acquisition metaphor (Sfard, 1998) is an unproductive way of viewing the learning and use of algorithms, but rather our development is offered as an opportunity to view algorithmic learning in a different way, that might further enlighten the field. In particular, we examine the use of horizontal and vertical mathematizing within the practice of algorithmatizing.

To illustrate, we summarize an example from the differential equations classroom teaching experiments. In a sequence of three activities, students worked on ways to estimate a solution to a differential equation, leading toward implementing Euler's method (Rasmussen & King, 2000). In the following discussion of horizontal and vertical mathematizing, we use the term "procedure" to indicate steps used to solve a particular task, and the term "algorithm" as a reference for a generalized procedure that is effective across a wide range of tasks.

Algorithmatizing: Horizontal Mathematizing

Instruction prior to the introduction of the following task focused on helping students conceptualize solutions to differential equations as functions, a notion that previous research had identified as needing development (Rasmussen, 2001). Students had also worked to develop a motivation for the reasonableness of a system of differential equations as a model of disease transmission in a closed system. After deriving this system of differential equations, the teacher presented the following task, adapted from Callahan and Hoffman (1995):

Consider a measles epidemic in a school population of 50,000 children. Suppose that 2,100 people are currently infected and 2,500 have already recovered. Use the following rate of change equations (time measured in days) to estimate the number of susceptible children (S), the number of infected children (I), and the number of recovered children (R) tomorrow and the next day. Organize your data in both tabular and graphical forms.

$$\frac{dS}{dt} = -.00001\,SI$$

$$\frac{dI}{dt} = .00001\,SI - \frac{I}{14}$$

$$\frac{dR}{dt} = \frac{1}{14}I$$

Students then engaged in a second task, that was grounded in a simpler situation involving fish in a lake. After an initial discussion to establish the reasonableness of the differential equation $\frac{dP}{dt} = kP$ to model unlimited growth of the fish, students engaged in the following task:

One way to model the growth of fish in a pond is with the differential equation $\frac{dP}{dt} = kP$, with time measured in years. Use this differential equation with a growth parameter $k = 1$ to approximate the number of fish in the pond for the next several years if there are initially (a) 200 fish, (b) 400 fish, and (c) 0 fish. Record your results in tabular and graphical forms.

Students were not supplied with any algorithms with which to approach the two problems. Rather, they had to figure out ways to use the rate of change equations to inform themselves about the quantities of interest. In this way, the mathematical idea of rate of change, together with the specific infectious disease or population scenario, serve as the context or ground from which students proceeded. This approach is in contrast to a traditional practice of first presenting the complete algorithm (Euler's method), with the expectation that students acquire the method and then apply it to a variety of problems. Because of the way in which the tasks were presented, students engaged in the practice of creating procedures for solving particular problems.

Students' efforts reflected their goals and purposes related to predicting future quantities such as the number of infected people or the population of fish. In the service of carrying out these goals, students enacted their understandings of rates of change to do calculations and created tables and graphs to help organize the information to answer questions about population growth or spread of disease. This particularity, the lack of generality of the students' procedures outside of the problem space they were given, is a characteristic of horizontal mathematizing, and forms a basis for a later shift to vertical mathematizing. With rate of change and the context situation as the ground for horizontally mathematizing the problem to develop a procedure, the students had a basis for developing algorithms, that represents a progression or advancement of their mathematical activity.

Algorithmatizing: Vertical Mathematizing

The final task in this sequence asked students to come up with a description (in words and equations) that might help another math or engineering student understand how to approximate the future number of fish in a pond with the differential equation $dP/dt = f(P)$, for some unknown expression $f(P)$. This task, of developing an algorithm, engaged students in the activity of reflecting on and generalizing their previous work. In this case, students began to consider situations in which the time increment need not be one unit and for a variety of types of functions $f(P)$. The procedure needed to be effective across these different situations, and not for a particular differential equation, initial condition, or increment of time. Thus, using their previous activity, students engaged in vertical mathematizing, allowing them to develop generalized formal algorithms.

The practice of developing an algorithm out of several experiences with particular cases represents a vertical mathematizing aspect of algorithmatizing. However, even the above task is set within the particular context of population growth. To move further along the mathematizing continuum, students may be given the following problem:

> Come up with a description (in words and equations) that might help another math or engineering student understand how to approximate a future value of the function $y(t)$ with the differential equation $dy/dt = f(t, y)$.

This task does not refer explicitly to y as a function describing a particular quantity of interest, nor is the differential equation autonomous.[4] Thus the task is intended to foster a further move toward generality.

The algorithm that students develop can then be the ground for further horizontal mathematizing. This happens when, for example, students are presented with particular situations in which they compare an exact solution to the approximate solution generated by their algorithm and they find that their algorithm does not provide reliable long-term predictions. This typically results in students creating explanations for why their algorithm behaves in the way it does in this particular

---

[4]An autonomous differential equation, dy/dt, is one that depends only on y.

case (horizontal mathematizing). In turn, such activity ultimately leads to their developing a better algorithm useful for all differential equations (vertical mathematizing). As this brief discussion illustrates, the practice of algorithmatizing, like symbolizing and defining, can often consist of more than one layer of horizontal and vertical mathematizing.

The mathematizing progression in this example is paradigmatic of the way in which mathematical activity continues to advance relative to students' previous mathematical activity. Students horizontally mathematized by beginning with a particular problem for which they developed a particular solution procedure. They then developed a generalized algorithm by extending, or vertically mathematizing, their previous activity with this procedure. These algorithms may then become the substance for further horizontal and vertical mathematizing activities. Although this example focuses on collegiate-level mathematics, the same ideas can be useful for elementary and secondary school mathematics. (See Campbell, Rowan, & Suarez, 1998, for an example of algorithmatizing in the early grades.)

DEFINING

Similar to symbolizing and algorithmatizing, the practice of defining can function both as an organizing activity (horizontal mathematizing) and as a means for generalizing, formalizing or creating a new mathematical reality (vertical mathematizing). Creating and using mathematical definitions, versus "everyday definitions," is an essential and often difficult activity for students, even those in upper-level courses such as real analysis (Edwards & Ward, 2004). Freudenthal (1973) distinguishes between two different types of defining activities in mathematics: descriptive and constructive. Descriptive defining "outlines a known object by singling out a few characteristic properties," whereas in constructive defining a person "models new objects out of familiar ones" (p. 457). We use this distinction to help us elaborate horizontal and vertical mathematizing in the domain of defining.

Defining: Horizontal Mathematizing

Descriptive defining is a type of organizing activity (i.e., it is an example of horizontal mathematizing). In a geometry classroom teaching experiment involving undergraduate mathematics, mathematics education, and computer science majors, we asked students to define a number of geometric concepts for which they already had a number of previous experiences in earlier mathematics courses. One of these was triangle. The small group and whole class discussions of possible definitions included arguments over whether the suggested definitions separated examples from nonexamples, whether trivial or extreme examples of triangles should be included, whether a suggested definition was as efficient as it could have been (i.e., did it include redundant characteristics? Should it?), and whether or not the suggested definition included terms that themselves should be defined before their use would be allowed.

These discussions helped clarify what a triangle should be and what criteria were necessary and sufficient to describe such a figure. This type of organizing and clarifying is consistent with what we term as horizontal mathematizing.[5] As we illustrate in the next section, this horizontal mathematizing activity, that in this case can be thought of as descriptive defining, served as the ground or context for activities we characterize as vertical mathematizing.

Defining: Vertical Mathematizing

In contrast to descriptive defining, that singles out characteristic properties of a known object, constructive defining creates new objects by building on and extending these known objects. In the same geometry teaching experiment, we invited students to interpret their planar triangle definition as a definition for triangle on a sphere. Students quickly realized that the only technical change needed was to interpret any mention of straight line in the planar definition as a great circle on the sphere. However, the activity of defining did not stop with this seemingly small change. Students elucidated the definition by creating numerous examples and arguing about whether an example such as the quarter sphere should be called a triangle. (A quarter sphere connects a pole and two antipodal equator points with great circles. Thus, the vertices are colinear, but the area of the figure is positive, unlike when one takes three colinear points on a plane.)

Students struggled to reconcile their planar images of triangle with the planar (now spherical) definition of triangle and the spherical images of possible triangles that they began to generate. This type of activity builds on the previous organizational activity, prompting generalization and abstraction as students use their definition to "define" and create this new concept for themselves through the activity of examining examples. Such defining activity begins to create a new mathematical reality for students—one that consists of new geometric objects and new mathematical relationships between these objects. Such generalizing and abstracting activity that builds on previous mathematizing fits our view of vertical mathematizing. A quote from the journal of a student named Peter captures this experience:

---

[5]The activity can also be analyzed from another perspective. Students were implicitly developing criteria for what constitutes a "definition." Thus, they were simultaneously engaged in horizontally mathematizing the process of defining as they created a concept definition specifically for "triangle." Edwards (1999) elaborates on this notion by analyzing the processes by which students create a concept image (Tall & Vinner, 1981) for mathematical definition.

From the figure [they had] drawn, it didn't seem like it was a figure at all, but in close observation it was a triangle! Yes, a triangle. It was a triangle based on the definition we chose in class. The definition of a triangle matched up with the figure. Though this was true, the figure did not look like a triangle. I did not see the triangle until someone brought up that it was a triangle by definition. Better yet, there were two triangles! Yes, the inside AND the outside were both triangles.

Students continued generalizing and abstracting as they made conjectures (without prompting from the teacher) about the properties of triangles on the sphere based on the examples that they generated. It is significant that students were generating conjectures about properties of spherical triangles without prompting from the teacher because it suggests that these students were pursuing their goals and purposes in relation to this new mathematical reality of the surface of the sphere. Moreover, this conjecturing process no longer referred back to planar triangles and continued to expand students' notions of spherical triangle, as reflected in another quote from Peter's journal:

Another surprising observation was when Group 1 gathered information about triangles on a sphere and concluded that the maximum number of degrees that a triangle can have with respect to its angles is 1080 [sic] degrees. These observations [have] changed my view on spheres. All along I was thinking and limited to a 2-dimensional perspective.

As these quotes illustrate, in constructive defining the majority of the elaboration of a concept lies beyond the initiation of the defining activity, beyond the writing or stating of the definition for the first time. In contrast, in descriptive defining the elaboration of the concept occurs primarily before the writing of the definition, hence writing or stating the definition occurs toward the end of the defining activity and the actual agreement on a definition within a certain social structure (e.g., the classroom) is the finishing touch to the defining activity.

The previous example illustrates how students may progress from horizontal to vertical mathematizing by using the organizing activities of horizontal mathematizing as a basis for vertical mathematizing. As illustrated next, such newly formed mathematical realities can become the ground for further mathematizing activity. For example, when investigating whether the condition that two spherical triangles having two sides and the included angle congruent necessarily means that the triangles are congruent, students created a new class of spherical triangles for which this theorem was true. They identified this new mathematical object as a "small triangle" with definitions that varied from group to group. Creating a new class of spherical triangles indicates that triangles on the sphere have become an object in their own right, for students, and the creating of small triangles represents horizontal mathematizing of their new world of spherical triangles. In addition, students considered the equivalence of these various definitions of small triangles and used small triangles as links in chains of deductive reasoning. These mathematizing activities are vertical in nature because they are more formal or abstract in relation to the starting point of defining a triangle on a plane, as well as in relation to their newly created realities of spherical triangles.

As this final example illustrates, advancing mathematical activity can involve more than one layer of horizontal and vertical mathematizing. Students' new mathematical realities (in this case, the world of spherical triangles) that resulted from their earlier mathematizing activities served as the ground for further mathematizing, creating a progressive mathematizing chain or sequence.

CONCLUSION

In the previous examples we developed the idea of advancing mathematical activity by focusing on the nature of students' participation in mathematical practices, elaborating horizontal and vertical mathematizing activities within the practices of symbolizing, algorithmatizing, and defining. Setting horizontal and vertical mathematical activity in relief against each other provides a way to characterize both the nature of students' activity and the progression of this activity. Horizontal and vertical mathematizing activities do not occur in isolation, but comprise a duality referred to as progressive mathematizing. The nature of the activity changes as students shift and slide between what we characterized as horizontal and vertical mathematizing. Horizontal mathematizing capitalizes on students' initial or informal ways of reasoning, with subsequent activities grounded in and building on this work. Participating in the practices of symbolizing, algorithmatizing, and defining facilitates progressive mathematization, generalizations, and the development of new mathematical realities.

It is important to keep in mind that horizontal and vertical mathematizing are of equal value and not intended to reflect some fundamental distinction in the quality or content of cognitive structures (cf. Schwingendorf, Hawks, & Beineke, 1992). Thus, regardless of whether students are learning about compactness or multiplication, the construct of advancing mathematical activity, with its attention to horizontal and vertical mathematizing, is potentially useful for researchers who want to document the development of different types of mathematical practices that emerge in classrooms and for teachers and curriculum developers who want to plan for students' mathematical growth. In particular, advancing mathematical activity via progressive mathematization offers a framework to view two of the three key aspects of what Simon (1995) refers to as a mathematical teaching cycle—the learning goals and a conjectured learning process.

The emphasis on activity, that involves both doing and thinking, resonates with a view of learning as participating in different practices that engage particular goals and purposes of those involved. Essential to the classroom teaching experiments from which we developed the construct of advancing mathematical activity was the fact that explicit attention was paid to explanation and justification. In particular, it became normative for students to routinely explain their thinking in whole class discussions, attempt to make sense of other students' thinking, and indicate agreement or disagreement with other students' mathematical ideas, interpretations, and conclusions. This provided an opportunity to gain insight into the changing nature of mathematical practices, resulting in the development of the notion of advancing mathematical activity.

At the beginning of the article we characterized mathematical learning as participating in mathematical practices. Although not exhaustive, symbolizing, algorithmatizing, and defining were tendered as important examples of such practices. We redirected the discussion on the nature of advanced mathematical thinking to that of advancing mathematical activity. We further put forward the notion of progressive mathematization, composed of horizontal and vertical mathematizing activities, as a means to develop the idea of advancing mathematical activity.

Next, we point to some links and parallels between the practices of symbolizing, algorithmatizing, and defining with respect to horizontal and vertical mathematizing. In the case of all three practices, an important commonality is the interplay between creating and using. The functions that creating and using serve in horizontal mathematizing, however, are different than in vertical mathematizing. In the practice of symbolizing, horizontal mathematizing involved creating a phase line as a record of student reasoning. In the example of algorithmatizing, horizontal mathematizing resulted in creating a procedure to provide future population estimates. In the defining example, creating definitions for planar triangle were an important part of the horizontal mathematizing. Creating the phase line, the procedure, and the definition were done in part to express, support, and communicate ideas that were more or less already familiar, ideas that connected with students' informal or current conceptions.

Further horizontal mathematizing involved using a phase line, using a procedure, and using a definition of triangle. This use, however, remained within the particulars of the problem situation. Using symbols, procedures, and definitions function differently in vertical mathematizing. Using serves the purpose of creating new mathematical realities. The creating in vertical mathematizing is therefore unlike the creating in horizontal mathematizing because, as we said earlier, creating the phase line, the procedure, and the definition were done in part to express, support, and communicate ideas that were more or less already familiar, as opposed to creating new mathematical realities.

Using the phase line, the procedure, and the definition in vertical mathematizing promoted movement from the particular to the more general and in some cases the more formal. In the symbolizing example, students used the phase line to explore the impact of varying a parameter. In the algorithmatizing example, students used their procedure for new and yet-to-be determined differential equations. In the defining example, students used their familiar definition on the not so (mathematically) familiar setting of the sphere. As we illustrated, these uses fostered and promoted the emergence of new mathematical realities for students.

Finally, to what extent might an instructional and curricular focus on advancing mathematical activity help ease what is often seen as a difficult transition "from a position where concepts have an intuitive basis founded on experience, to one where they are specified by formal definitions and their properties reconstructed through logical deductions" (Tall, 1992, p. 495)? This transition is indeed difficult when students' intuitive basis founded on experience is an island (Kaput, 1994) separated from their reasoning based on formal definitions and logical deductions. In contrast to a separation of reasoning, the construct of advancing mathematical activity offers teachers, instructional designers, and researchers a practice-oriented way to think about the transition from informal to more formal mathematical reasoning.

ACKNOWLEDGMENTS

Support for this article was funded in part by the National Science Foundation under grants No. REC–9875388 and REC–0093494. The opinions expressed do not necessarily reflect the views of the foundation. The authors thank members of the PME–NA Advanced Mathematical Thinking Group at the Tucson meeting for their suggestions and comments, in particular: Julia Aguirre, Virginia Bastable, Apple Bloom, Sally Jacobs, Dave Klanderman, Mike Oehrtman, Nikita Patterson, Angela Teachey, and Pat Wilson. We also thank Joan Ferrini-Mundy, Annie and John Selden, and two anonymous reviewers for their comments on an earlier draft of this article.

REFERENCES

Berlinski, D. (2000). *The advent of the algorithm: The idea that rules the world.* New York: Harcourt.
Blanchard, P., Devaney, R., & Hall, R. (1998). *Differential equations.* Boston: Brooks/Cole.
Callahan, J., & Hoffman, K. (1995). *Calculus in context.* New York: W. H. Freeman and Company.
Campbell, P. F., Rowan, T. E., & Suarez, A. R. (1998). What criteria for student-invented algorithms? In L. J. Morrow & M. J. Kenney (Eds.), *The teaching and learning of algorithms in school mathematics* (pp. 49–55). Reston, VA: National Council of Teachers of Mathematics.
Cobb, P. (2000). Conducting teaching experiments in collaboration with teachers. In A. E. Kelly & R. A. Lesh (Eds.), *Handbook of research design in mathematics and science education* (pp. 307–333). Mahwah, NJ: Lawrence Erlbaum Associates, Inc.

Cobb, P., & Bowers, J. (1999). Cognitive and situated learning perspectives in theory and practice. *Educational Researcher, 28*(2), 4–15.

Cobb, P., & Yackel, E. (1996). Constructivist, emergent, and sociocultural perspectives in the context of developmental research. *Educational Psychologist, 31*(3/4), 175–190.

Dewey, J. (1991). *How we think.* Buffalo, NY: Prometheus Books. (Original work published 1910)

Edwards, B. (1999). Revisiting the notion of concept image/concept definition. In F. Hitt & M. Santos (Eds.), *Proceedings of the 21st Annual Meeting of the North American Chapter of the International Group for the Psychology of Mathematics Education* (Vol. 1, pp. 205–210). Columbus, OH: ERIC Clearinghouse for Science, Mathematics, and Environmental Education.

Edwards, B. S., & Ward, M. B. (2004). Surprises from mathematics education research: Student (mis)use of mathematical definitions. *The American Mathematical Monthly, 111*(5), 411–424.

Freudenthal, H. (1973). *Mathematics as an educational task.* Dordrecht, The Netherlands: Reidel.

Freudenthal, H. (1991). *Revisiting mathematics education.* Dordrecht, The Netherlands: Kluwer Academic.

Gravemeijer, K. (1994). *Developing realistic mathematics education.* Utrecht, The Netherlands: CD-b Press.

Gravemeijer, K. (1999). How emergent models may foster the constitution of formal mathematics. *Mathematical Thinking and Learning, 1,* 155–177.

Gravemeijer, K., Cobb, P., Bowers, J., & Whitenack, J. (2000). Symbolizing, modeling, and instructional design. In P. Cobb, E. Yackel, & K. McClain (Eds.), *Symbolizing and communication in mathematics classrooms: Perspectives on discourse, tools, and instructional design* (pp. 225–273). Mahwah, NJ: Lawrence Erlbaum Associates, Inc.

Herscovics, N. (1996). The construction of conceptual schemes in mathematics. In L. Steffe, P. Nesher, P. Cobb, G. Goldin, & B. Greer (Eds.), *Theories of mathematical learning* (pp. 351–379). Mahwah, NJ: Lawrence Erlbaum Associates, Inc.

Kaput, J. (1994). The representational roles of technology in connecting mathematics with authentic experience. In R. Biehler, R. W. Scholz, R. Straber, & B. Winkelmann (Eds.), *Didactics of mathematics as a scientific discipline* (pp. 379–397). Dordrecht, The Netherlands: Kluwer Academic.

Lave, J., & Wenger, E. (1991). *Situated learning: Legitimate peripheral participation.* Cambridge, UK: Cambridge University Press.

Meira, L. (1995). The microevolution of mathematical representations in children's activity. *Cognition and Instruction, 13,* 269–313.

Nemirovsky, R. (1994). On ways of symbolizing: The case of Laura and the velocity sign. *Journal of Mathematical Behavior, 13,* 389–422.

Pirie, S., & Kieren, T. (1994). Growth in mathematical understanding: How can we characterise it and how can we represent it? *Educational Studies in Mathematics, 26,* 61–86.

Rasmussen, C. (1999, April). *Symbolizing and unitizing in support of students' mathematical growth in differential equations.* Paper presented at the Annual Meeting of the National Council of Teachers of Mathematics Research Presession, San Francisco, CA.

Rasmussen, C. (2001). New directions in differential equations: A framework for interpreting students' understandings and difficulties. *Journal of Mathematical Behavior, 20,* 55–87.

Rasmussen, C., & King, K. (2000). Locating starting points in differential equations: A realistic mathematics approach. *International Journal of Mathematical Education in Science and Technology, 31,* 161–172.

Rasmussen, C., Yackel, E., & King, K. (2003). Social and sociomathematical norms in the mathematics classroom. In R. Charles (Ed.), *Teaching mathematics through problem solving: It's about learning mathematics* (pp. 143–154). Reston, VA: National Council of Teachers of Mathematics.

Schwingendorf, K., Hawks, J., & Beineke, J. (1992). Horizontal and vertical growth of the students' conception of function. In G. Harel & E. Dubinsky (Eds.), *The concept of function: Aspects of epistemology and pedagogy* (pp. 133–149). Washington, DC: Mathematical Association of America.

Sfard, A. (1998). On two metaphors for learning and the dangers of choosing just one. *Educational Researcher, 27*(2), 4–13.

Simon, M. A. (1995). Reconstructing mathematics pedagogy from a constructivist perspective. *Journal for Research in Mathematics Education, 26*, 114–145.

Stephan, M., & Rasmussen, C. (2002). Classroom mathematical practices in differential equations. *Journal of Mathematical Behavior, 21,* 459–490.

Tall, D. (1991). The psychology of advanced mathematical thinking. In D. Tall (Ed.), *Advanced mathematical thinking* (pp. 3–21). Dordrecht, The Netherlands: Kluwer Academic.

Tall, D. (1992). The transition to advanced mathematical thinking: Functions, limits, infinity and proof. In D. A. Grouws (Ed.), *Handbook of research on mathematics teaching and learning* (pp. 495–511). New York: Macmillan.

Tall, D., & Vinner, S. (1981). Concept image and concept definition in mathematics with particular reference to limits and continuity. *Educational Studies in Mathematics, 12*, 151–169.

Treffers, A. (1987). *Three dimensions. A model of goal and theory description in mathematics education: The Wiskobas project.* Dordrecht, The Netherlands: Kluwer Academic.

Wenger, E. (1998). *Communities of practice: Learning, meaning, and identity.* Cambridge, UK: Cambridge University Press.

Yackel, E., Rasmussen, C., & King, K. (2000). Social and sociomathematical norms in an advanced undergraduate mathematics course. *Journal of Mathematical Behavior, 19*, 275–287.

ENGAGING YOUNG CHILDREN IN MATHEMATICS

Standards for Early Childhood Mathematics Education
Edited by

Douglas H. Clements, Julie Sarama
State University of New York/College at Buffalo
Associate Editor: Ann-Marie DiBiase
Brock University
A Volume in the Studies in Mathematical Thinking and Learning Series

"This work fills a tremendous vacuum that has existed for many years, taking a close look at early mathematics teaching and learning in a way that reflects both the early childhood and mathematics education perspectives. It should be useful for virtually anyone with a serious interest in early mathematics learning. Two thumbs up!"
—W. Gary Martin,
Auburn University

Engaging Young Children in Mathematics: Standards for Early Childhood Mathematics Education brings together the combined wisdom of a diverse group of experts involved with early childhood mathematics. The book originates from the landmark 2000 Conference on Standards for Pre-kindergarten and Kindergarten Mathematics Education, attended by representatives from almost every state developing standards for young children's mathematics; federal government officials; mathematicians; mathematics educators; researchers from mathematics education, early childhood education, and psychology; curriculum developers; teachers; policy makers; and professionals from organizations such as the National Conference of Teachers of Mathematics and the National Association for the Education of Young Children. The main goal of the Conference was to work collectively to help those responsible for framing and implementing early childhood mathematics standards. Although it has its roots in the Conference, the expanded scope of the standards and recommendations covered in this book includes the full range of kindergarten to grade 2.

The volume is organized into two main parts and an online appendix (**http://www.gse.buffalo.edu/ org/conference/**). Part One, *Major Themes and Recommendations*, offers a framework for thinking about pre-kindergarten - grade 2 mathematics education and specific recommendations. Part Two, *Elaboration of Major Themes and Recommendations*, provides substantive detail regarding young students' understandings of mathematical ideas. Each Part includes five parallel subsections: "Standards in Early Childhood Education"; "Mathematics Standards and Guidelines"; "Curriculum, Learning, Teaching, and Assessment"; "Professional Development"; and "Toward the Future: Implementation and Policy." As a whole the book:
* presents comprehensive summaries of research that provide specific guidelines for standards, curriculum, and teaching;
* takes the recent reports and recommendations for early childhood mathematics education to the next level;
* integrates practical details and research throughout; and
* provides a succinct, but thorough review of research on the topics, sequences, and learning trajectories that children can and should learn at each of their first years of life, with specific developmental guidelines that suggest appropriate content for each topic for each year from 2-year-olds to 7-year-olds.

This is an indispensable volume for mathematics educators, researchers, curriculum developers, teachers and policy makers, including those who create standards, scope and sequences, and curricula for young children and professional teacher development materials, and students in mathematics education, early childhood trainers, teacher educators, and faculty in mathematics education.
0-8058-4210-1 [cloth] / 2004 / 488pp. / $99.95
0-8058-4534-8 [paper] / 2004 / 488pp. / $49.95
Prices are subject to change without notice.

COMPLETE TABLE OF CONTENTS AVAILABLE AT **www.erlbaum.com**

Lawrence Erlbaum Associates, Inc.
10 Industrial Ave., Mahwah, NJ 07430–2262
201–258–2200; 1–800–926–6579; fax 201–760–3735
orders@erlbaum.com; www.erlbaum.com

2005 SUBSCRIPTION ORDER FORM

MATHEMATICAL THINKING AND LEARNING

AN INTERNATIONAL JOURNAL

Volume 7, 2005, Quarterly — ISSN 1098–6065/Online ISSN 1532–7833

SUBSCRIPTION PRICES PER VOLUME:

Please ❑ enter ❑ renew my subscription:

Category:	Access Type:	Price: US-Canada/All Other Countries
❑ Individual	Online & Print	$60.00/$90.00

Subscriptions are entered on a calendar-year basis only and must be paid in advance in U.S. currency—check, credit card, or money order. Prices for subscriptions include postage and handling. **Journal prices expire 12/31/05.** NOTE: Institutions must pay institutional rates. Individual subscription orders are welcome if prepaid by credit card or personal check. **Please note:** A $20.00 penalty will be charged against customers providing checks that must be returned for payment. This assessment will be made only in instances when problems in collecting funds are directly attributable to customer error.

❑ **Check Enclosed** (U.S. Currency Only)   **Total Amount Enclosed $**_____

❑ **Charge My:** ❑ VISA ❑ MasterCard ❑ AMEX ❑ Discover

Card Number _____   Exp. Date_____/_____

Signature_____
(Credit card orders cannot be processed without your signature.)
PRINT CLEARLY for proper delivery. STREET ADDRESS/SUITE/ROOM # REQUIRED FOR DELIVERY.

Name_____

Address_____

City/State/Zip+4_____

Daytime Phone #_____E-mail address_____
Prices are subject to change without notice. **Direct all inquiries and orders to the address below.**

For information about online subscriptions, visit our website at *www.LEAonline.com*

LIBRARY RECOMMENDATION FORM

DETACH AND FORWARD TO YOUR LIBRARIAN.

❑ I have reviewed the description of *MTL* and would like to recommend it for acquisition.

MATHEMATICAL THINKING AND LEARNING

AN INTERNATIONAL JOURNAL

Volume 7, 2005, Quarterly — ISSN 1098–6065/Online ISSN 1532–7833

Category:	Access Type:	Price: US-Canada/All Other Countries
❑ Institutional	Online & Print	$440.00/$470.00
❑ Institutional	Online Only	$395.00/$395.00
❑ Institutional	Print Only	$420.00/$450.00

Name_____Title_____

Institution/Department_____

Address_____

E-mail Address_____
Librarians, please send your orders directly to LEA or contact from your subscription agent.

DIRECT ALL SUBSCRIPTION ORDERS TO:
Lawrence Erlbaum Associates, Inc.,
Journal Subscription Department; 10 Industrial Avenue, Mahwah, NJ 07430
(201) 258–2200; FAX (201) 760–3735; journals@erlbaum.com

LEA LAWRENCE ERLBAUM ASSOCIATES

LEA Online
WWW.LEAONLINE.COM

CLASSROOM COMMUNICATION AND DIVERSITY

Enhancing Instructional Practice

Robert G. Powell,
Dana Caseau
California State University, Fresno
A Volume in LEA's Communication Series

Teachers face myriad communication challenges in today's classroom, reflecting the growing diversity of the student body; the ever-increasing number of students; gender issues; and students' learning disabilities. This volume provides a useful framework for helping new and experienced teachers manage the diverse communication challenges they encounter. It also encourages teachers to reflect on how their personal cultures influence their expectations about appropriate classroom communication and ways to demonstrate learning.

This textbook is distinctive in its integration of information from a variety of sources to establish a viewpoint that focuses on the needs of the individual learner. Drawing on the research in the communication and education disciplines, authors Robert G. Powell and Dana Caseau provide theoretical models and useful strategies for improving instructional practices. They address the ways in which culture influences communication in the classroom, and assist teachers in developing the skills necessary to meet the needs of the students in their classrooms.

Much of the information shared in this text derives from the authors' research and experience in schools and from the experiences of others, including teachers, parents, and children. Their experiences, combined with the cross-disciplinary approach, produce a volume of unique perspectives and considerable insight. Teachers and scholars in the communication and education disciplines will find this text to be a practical and valuable tool for classroom teaching, and it is appropriate for instructional communication courses in the areas of communication and education.

Contents: Preface. Introduction. Communication and the Classroom. Factors Influencing Learning and Communication. Diversity and Classroom Communication. Gender and Classroom Communication. Students With Special Needs. Building Relationships. Building a Community of Learners. Behavioral Management. Instructional Strategies. Technology and Instructional Communication.
0-8058-4025-7 [cloth] / 2004 / 256pp. / $59.95
0-8058-4026-5 [paper] / 2004 / 256pp. / $29.95
Prices are subject to change without notice.

Lawrence Erlbaum Associates, Inc.
10 Industrial Ave., Mahwah, NJ 07430–2262
201–258–2200; 1–800–926–6579; fax 201–760–3735
orders@erlbaum.com; www.erlbaum.com

LESSON STUDY

A Japanese Approach to Improving Mathematics
Teaching and Learning

Clea Fernandez
Columbia University

Makoto Yoshida
Global Education Resources

A Volume in the Studies in Mathematical Thinking and Learning Series

*"Clea Fernandez and Makoto Yoshida have made major contributions
to our understanding of lesson study, and this book clearly is one of
the most important of these. They tell the story of lesson study at one
school in a way that is accurate and true to Japanese practice, yet
accessible and comprehensible to U.S. audiences....This book presents
the details of Japanese lesson study, and these details can take your
breath away....Those of us interested in lesson study, and in improving teaching and learning in U.S.
schools, should be grateful for the care and clarity with which Clea Fernandez and Makoto Yoshida
have presented the substance of Japanese lesson study. There is much learned in these pages."*
                                                                              —James. W. Stigler
                                        University of California at Los Angeles, From the Foreword

Lesson study is a popular professional development approach in Japan whereby teachers
collaborate to study content, instruction, and how students solve problems and reach
for understanding in order to improve elementary mathematics instruction and learning
in the classroom.

This book is the first comprehensive look at the system and process of lesson study in
Japan. It describes in detail the process of how teachers conducted lesson study—how
they collaborated in order to develop a lesson, what they talked about during the process,
and what they looked at in order to understand deeply how students were learning.
Readers see the planning of a mathematics lesson, as well as how much content
knowledge the teachers have. They observe students' problem solving strategies and
learn how Japanese teachers prepare themselves to identify those strategies and facilitate
the students' discussion.

Written for mathematics teachers, educational researchers, school administrators
interested in teachers' professional development, and professional developers, this
landmark volume provides an in-depth understanding of lesson study that can lead to
positive changes in teachers' professional development and in teaching and learning in
the United States.

Contents: J.W. Stigler, Foreword. Introduction. An Overview of Lesson Study. Lesson Study
at Tsuta Elementary School. Illustrating the Lesson Study Through the Work of Five Tsuta
Teachers. Drawing Up a Preliminary Lesson Plan. Refining the Lesson Plan. Preparing to
Teach the Study Lesson. Teaching the Study Lesson. Discussing How to Improve the Study
Lesson. The Revised Lesson Plan. Teaching the Revised Lesson. Sharing Reflections About
the Study Lesson. Follow-Up Activities: Sharing and Reflecting. Strategies for Avoiding Isolation in Order to Enhance Lesson Study. Conclusion. **Appendices.**
0-8058-3961-5 [cloth] / 2004 / 304pp. / $59.95
0-8058-3962-3 [paper] / 2004 / 304pp. / $29.95
Prices are subject to change without notice.

Lawrence Erlbaum Associates, Inc.
10 Industrial Ave., Mahwah, NJ 07430–2262
201–258–2200; 1–800–926–6579; fax 201–760–3735
orders@erlbaum.com; www.erlbaum.com

COGNITION AND CHANCE
The Psychology of Probabilistic Reasoning
Raymond S. Nickerson
Tufts University

"I liked this book a lot. I think that Nickerson has done a fine job in putting together coherently a wide range of material, which with the awarding of the Nobel Prize to Daniel Kahneman, has become an even hotter area. Thus this book is remarkably well timed."
—Dr. Howard Wainer
Distinguished Research Scientist,
National Board of Medical Examiners

"It is comprehensive in its approach to scholarship and does not choose a single point of view from among the usual ones. Instead, it offers wise and clever comments on the many different perspectives that exist."
—Dr. Jonathan Baron
Professor of Psychology, *University of Pennsylvania*

"The author is acknowledged as a clear and interesting writer. The present work is consistent with that reputation."
—Dr. Michael J. Wenger
Department of Psychology, *University of Notre Dame*

The ability to think probabilistically is important for many reasons. Lack of it makes one prone to a variety of irrational fears and vulnerable to scams designed to exploit probabilistic naivet'e, precludes intelligent assessment of risks, impairs decision making under uncertainty, facilitates the misinterpretation of statistical information, precludes critical evaluation of likelihood claims, and generally undercuts rational thinking in numerous ways. *Cognition and Chance* presents an overview of the information needed to avoid such pitfalls and to assess and respond to probabilistic situations in a rational way.

In this book, Dr. Nickerson investigates such questions as how good individuals are at thinking probabilistically and how consistent their reasoning under uncertainty is with principles of mathematical statistics and probability theory. He reviews evidence that has been produced in researchers' attempts to investigate these and similar types of questions. Seven conceptual chapters address such topics as probability, chance, randomness, coincidences, inverse probability, paradoxes, dilemmas, and statistics. The remaining five chapters focus on empirical studies of individuals' abilities and limitations as probabilistic thinkers. Topics include estimation and prediction, perception of covariation, choice under uncertainty, and people as intuitive probabilists.

Cognition and Chance is intended to appeal to researchers and students in the areas of probability, statistics, psychology, business, economics, decision theory, and social dilemmas.

Contents: Foreword. Probability and Chance. Randomness. Coincidences. Inverse Probability. Some Instructive Problems. Paradoxes and Dilemmas. Statistics. Estimation and Prediction. Perception of Covariation. Choice Under Uncertainty. People as Intuitive Probabilists. Concluding Comments.
0-8058-4898-3 [cloth] / 2004 / 536pp. / $110.00
0-8058-4899-1 [paper] / 2004 / 536pp. / $49.95
Prices are subject to change without notice.

Lawrence Erlbaum Associates, Inc.
10 Industrial Ave., Mahwah, NJ 07430–2262
201–258–2200; 1–800–926–6579; fax 201–760–3735
orders@erlbaum.com; www.erlbaum.com